BREAKING COMMON GROUND

DAILY THOUGHTS FOR A DIVIDED SOCIETY

JOHN L. WALKER, M.S., LPC

www.truebearingspress.com

© 2024 by John L. Walker

All rights reserved. No part of this book may be reproduced or transmitted in any form or by any means, electronic or mechanical, without prior written consent and permission from True Bearings Press.

Published by True Bearings Press
www.truebearingspress.com

ISBN 979-8-9916625-0-5

Dedication

To my wonderful wife Glenda. So many things would not be possible without your support. I love you!

In memory of Uly, a great dog.

Introduction

If you are reading this book, you are likely one of a growing group of Americans who are exhausted by our political divisions. This partitioning of society seems to be everywhere as we increasingly develop our personas along "red" and "blue" lines. This social phenomenon, while on its face benign enough, is becoming increasingly entrenched and is gaining practical importance. Its lines in the sand are becoming increasingly absolute, and its extremes are seen as calls to negative action. The split is becoming impossible to ignore, as large numbers even see the fissures as a potential cause for civil war along party lines. Past generations would have viewed the verbalizing of this as unthinkable, but the paradigm seems all too real and is becoming a frightening specter within the national psyche.

If you are here, it is also likely that you have not entirely given up on the notion of reconciliation. You probably still view kindness, reason, and common sense as transcendent agents that can foster change. Despite growing evidence to the contrary, you believe in common bonds as both humans and as Americans. Even if we cannot get on the same page politically, you separate this from the existential and affirm that we are not yet headed for oblivion.

This book is an attempt to provide support on a personal level for this feeling among those who want to participate in a solution. I believe the steps taken by each of us on an individual level matter greatly. I also think that the practice of facing one another and working to create satisfactory circumstances and relationships must be a daily endeavor. Toward this end, I have presented 365 thoughts about how we might accomplish this, one per day for an entire year. Each entry begins with a prompt regarding our feelings of division. It goes on to offer thoughts about each one and the need for change. I then propose an action that we can take today to move closer to unity.

This structure is loosely based on the psychological tenets of cognitive behavior theory. At its core is the belief that feelings, thoughts, and actions are interconnected. If we can change one, we can influence the others. These pages are my humble attempt to activate these principles in our public discourse. I hope we can restore societal feelings of civility and unity, one mindset and one interaction at a time.

I have done my best to be neutral in writing these entries. Their meaning, however, is ultimately viewed through the reader's lens. If you disagree with parts, please continue to read until you discover something of value to implement. I have also tried not to be too repetitive, but themes will likely emerge for you. If they do, please take them to heart for future use.

Please use this text as your daily assistant as you attempt to bring about change. Let it be your emotional companion and an impetus to continue your thinking and acting processes. I'm glad you are here!

1

Can We Still Have Harmony?

Is a middle ground between us a lost cause? Have we gone too far pushing ends further apart? Have we let extremism steal our ability to live in peace? Can we still find a way to understand others and the sum of their experiences, even if they differ from our own? Stepping into the middle ground does not mean that we have abandoned principles but that we are willing to accept humanity in others. Moving toward this with intent can heal wounds and explain the past actions of others, whether they are just or not.

Today, I will turn toward harmony for its power as a healer.

2

Truth as a Moving Target

Our society is full of different ways to gain information. Manufactured facts can support almost any version of the truth, and our division thrives on this. The road to unity insists that we identify genuine facts with honesty and hold onto them to address the common good.

Today, I will seek to understand accurate notions that will be useful in creating a better society.

3

Be Less Confrontational

The modern world is full of strong opinions. Feeling as though we are on the side of right somehow empowers us to be disrespectful. Each disagreement is not a need for confrontation. Generally, more can be solved by gently remaining in the middle as opposed to pushing our thoughts on others.

Today, I will strive to be less adversarial.

Common Ground

Striving to be right can lead us to ignore the experiences and thoughts of others. We tend to think of opinions as a zero-sum game. They drive our emotions and leave us with no middle ground upon which to meet others, build consensus, and offer solutions. Extremism seems to eschew common sense and drive us to our respective poles with no room for compromise or growth.

__Today, I will work to establish a solid common footing.__

Habits of Prejudice

An "us or them" mentality drives us to reinforce prejudices that have existed for years in our society. We tend to discount what we do not understand about the lives of people who have different backgrounds from us. These maladies have been cemented by a lack of thought and a lack of clear judgment. At times we are reflexive, delivering an evil undercurrent that has been instilled in us by our society and years of latent ill thought and behavior. Better mindfulness can prevent divisiveness.

Today, I will work to take the extra moment necessary to break old habits regarding my fellow human beings.

Science Versus Faith

Science and faith are not opposing propositions. While science can explain the way our world works and give us guidance about it, faith can provide answers where no logical straight line exists. The role of a Creator or Higher Power need not be excluded from those things that are driven by our planet and its rules of existence. Science, faith, and common sense can coexist to develop a more rational whole that accounts for the gray areas.

Today, I will work to understand and give away those things I do not understand.

7

Compassion

Existence is not always a battle where the winner takes all. We get caught in our own bubble, and the plight of others is not always at the front of our consciousness. We often don't see that love is a universal language that transcends culture, power, wealth, and circumstance. We can lift each other up with the same amount of energy we use to put people down. Even those that we disagree with are entitled to the power of love.

Today, I will place compassion at the front of my mind.

Let Go of the Past

Yesterday is history, and tomorrow is a mystery. Our mistakes tend to weigh us down and prevent us from moving on to better things. Too often, others show us our failings or remind us of times when we were less than loving or less than fair. This is a trap. This sort of thinking leaves us with nowhere better to turn. The faults of our fathers don't have to be ours.

Today, I will do my best to move forward and help others to move forward.

9

Religion as a Divider

I was commenting to someone the other day that "there is so much evil done in the name of the Lord." Religious traditions leave us unwilling to compromise, as we feel that it is "our way or the highway" based upon the authority given to us by the Supreme. The apparent wages of disbelief in a particular dogma are often doom and injury.

Today, I will concentrate on the true meaning of my faith and work to use it to lift and inspire others.

10

Those Things That Defy Logic

At opposite poles, a sort of "herd mentality" has taken hold, which ignores rational thought. The most outlandish explanations, the least understandable path seem to be the order of the day. As opposed to conspiring and concocting to explain bad events, the path to common ground flows through an analytical search for truth. Only then can logic yield to faith to bring us to a workable consensus. It allows us to cross the finish line to better outcomes.

Today, I will not lend credence to narratives that leave common sense behind.

Sincere Patriotism

Patriotism seems to have come to mean a proprietary point of view in our society. Instead of being all-inclusive, it sometimes passes for divisive politics where only one side can claim to be true disciples. Generations before us have fought for the right to express opposing opinions. It is the sort of patriotism that gave us the very right to be divergent. Being a patriot is in support of that heritage and not any one ideology.

Today, I will honor the true meaning of being patriotic.

Working with Voices in the Darkness

Political discourse, when at its most contentious, can make us feel that all is lost and that no one can agree on anything. It can feel like a freight train headed over the edge of a cliff. Even amid extremism, unity insists that we listen closely and look for even the smallest element of commonality. It is the singular building block from which we can work for a change of direction.

Today, I will do my best to look for even the slightest common ground where none seems to exist.

13

Who Is Watching?

Division seems to have become a way of life. We engage in it without thinking about the legacy it leaves. Hatred is generational, an awful legacy we pass down to our children. Kindness is also the same sort of generational force. We can be part of the solution to the things that separate us.

Today, I will work toward being a good example.

14

Why Do They Believe It?

We can look across the divide and see that others have wildly different ideas. We may not, however, have a clear picture of how they arrived at them. Each one of us has our own experiences, and they shape the outcome. Each of us has a right to our background, to be the sum of our learning. We do not, however, have the right to force the will of our beliefs on an entire society.

Today, I will respect the origins of the thoughts of others.

15

End of the Name-Calling

Name-calling drives a wedge between us. It is the laziest form of disrespect. It takes no time to understand the quality or character of what we perceive cynically to be inferior. Instead, it is the shorthand that hatred uses. It cuts deeply. As much as we try, we cannot ignore the wounds. They are an evil stream that erodes the shores, pushing us farther apart.

Today, I will be mindful to refer to others with care.

Consider Goodwill

Divisive, adversarial relationships seem to be everywhere in this age of "me against them" rhetoric. We build walls. The mortar hardens with each passing snub, a roll of the eye, and a smear of others. Altruism is the salve that heals wounds, reaches across, and humanizes. It is easier to practice than we think. It is the beginning of listening, loving, and forgiving.

Today, I will work to make gentle regard for others my default.

17

Magical Thinking

Magical thinking is an enigma. At its worst, it ignores facts and creates a narrative that fits lust for power and justifies our fears. At its best, it becomes the basis for the sort of curiosity that drives science forward. At its most useful, however, it is the core of spirituality. It explains the things we cannot explain and is a place of refuge when the logical mind can no longer carry us to wisdom. Humanity moves forward when there is a balance, free of agenda.

Today, I will be a voice for balance between science and the spiritual world.

Misplacing Duty

Duty is comprised of perceived obligations. It drives us to complete the moral contract we have made with society. It helps us maintain order and persevere in putting individual wants aside for the common good. Duty goes astray when it breaks our internal sense of right and wrong and is used as a panacea to justify our participation in evil brought to bear on others. These are the moral injuries that undermine us and tear away at the well-being of our souls.

Today, I will balance duty with my internal truth.

Accept the Ideas of Others at Face Value

An exchange of ideas fosters the best workable solutions. Accepting the input of others without looking for a deeper agenda may present a way through difficulty. Deeper motives may exist. If we at least initially listen without judging, however, we have the benefit of complete information. We make way for faster resolutions, enhanced results, and more profound peace.

Today, I will absorb the ideas of others and not reject them out of hand.

Can We Celebrate Differences?

Polarization in our politics seems to have left us less room to celebrate different points of view, different ethnicities, and different past experiences. Diversity was one of the cornerstones upon which our country was founded, welcoming all who would come to our shores. While we can be proud of our country, we should also be aware that our way is not the only way. Our founding fathers were misfits who left another country to be free. The same is true today for many attempting to come to our country for a better way of life.

Today, I will be mindful of differences and respectful of others.

21

Banners of Hatred

Ancient banners of hatred and distrust still fly among us. No matter how others justify their animus with rationalizations of how they have benign meaning in the current day, they remain the symbol of past atrocity. They bring evil forward and do not allow it to die.

Today, I will remove symbols of hate from my life and ask others to do so.

Concentrate Through the Noise

Our media seem to have descended into hyperbole and divisive clashing agendas. The twenty-four-hour news cycle has, in its lust for content, created chaos and discord. Instead of conveying facts to stand on their merit with each of us, they are presented with a slant that moves discord forward. It has become a wasteland where we are spoon-fed hateful agendas at worst and left not knowing where to place our trust at best. Even more than this, the information age has given us so many ways to allegedly verify facts that we can contort even the most outlandish claims into a seemingly straight line to authenticity. It is up to each of us to discover an objective truth, ignoring the forces that would keep us away from it.

Today, I will discover my own verifiable truth about current events.

Be Part of the Solution

The poles of discord perpetuate themselves. We divide and seek to conquer others we do not agree with or understand. We are content to keep pushing further apart to the exclusion of innovative ideas and new means of identifying and solving problems that would bring us together for common advancement. We do this in the name of winning for our side. Why can't we all win?

Today, I will look for the middle ground and focus on solutions and not victory.

Beyond the Pale

Today's political discourse seems to be finding new contentious territory. The thoughts, actions, and intransigence can be staggering and surprising as we wonder what might come next. Yesterday's norms seem thrown out the window as bewildering new precedents are set. As those seeking unity, we must be willing to synthesize these occurrences in the light of the shock value they are intended to inflict and forge places where they can be understood and mitigated.

Today, I will work not to be shocked by events and simply move forward despite them.

What Are We Teaching?

Those of us willing to find the middle ground must seize learning experiences that highlight the best of what we would have our children learn of love, honor, and dignity. We must seek to eliminate the bad and reinforce the good. Only in this way can we ensure a legacy that builds up instead of tearing down.

Today, I will seek to be mindful of the messages I leave behind.

Sometime Within a Million Years

Circumstances dictate to us that the road to unity must be followed with urgency. While our division has not come to us overnight, bad results loom ominous and can threaten our very existence. Time compresses, and the very speed of modern culture moves us rapidly closer to irreversible damage. The only plausible solution is to prioritize our movement toward rapid decision-making and a common ground that will inspire everyone to action.

Today, I will strive to impress upon others that time is a moving force but that it is not too late to create a better future together.

27

What Else Is There to Talk About?

Boredom is dangerous, and ignorance tends to try to fill a void and cause us to speak the first thing that is present in our minds. We are not as satisfied with silence as we could be. Mindless group mentality has a chance to take over. When this happens, we find ourselves unable to make small talk without taking a hard turn to the perceived faults of others. We have a pat monologue ready that is replete with talking points and spoon-feedings. We become parrots, promoting what are likely the misunderstandings of the day about each other. We can avoid this with mindful intent.

Today, let me speak of subjects that reinforce good and show others peace.

Remove Labels

Our divisive times have placed our fellow humans in convenient classifications. They are shorthand for what we think we know about others. With the convenience that we have come to expect from absolutely everything, they seek to save us time in thought and allow us to simply act on the basest of assumptions. It is way too easy to criticize and move on than to think, consider, and then act. Too many mistakes happen.

Today, I will attempt not to see others as labels but as individuals.

29

Wrapping My Head Around Hatred

Peace soothes. Hatred slices. It is the sharpest cut, leaves the deepest wounds, and removes hope. Why do so many people speak of hate? I suspect that this impression comes from the scores of people who use the word when the emotions of the situation shouldn't be that strong. It's the proverbial "nuclear option." It is way too powerful to occupy any place in the slang vocabulary of our culture.

Today, I will not use the language of hate. I will measure my words in order to unite and not divide.

Honor Others

Our society was founded on the premise that everyone has intrinsic worth. While mutual regard seems hard to come by in troubled times, we must practice it in a way that preserves common bonds. We must bow to each other with a reverent spirit and an open heart.

Today, I will work to see the good in others and value it.

Souls Under Repair

I am a talk therapist, and one theme runs through most of my work with others. Over time, more than one client has expressed that their "soul is tired." This describes the weariness of polarization that seems to exist in society at large and manifests itself in our own experiences. It feels defeatist, all-powerful, and final. This does not have to be permanent, however. We can rejuvenate ourselves a little at a time. We can face inward, seek truth, and allow tolerance.

Today, I will concentrate on repairing the injury my soul has sustained at the hands of others and in the absence of my complete understanding.

Beauty Doesn't Pick Sides

The Grand Canyon is one of the most beautiful spots on Earth. It is wonderous and majestic and suggests a power and being beyond us. Its visitors are forever changed. It is worth noting that this grandeur is not male or female, straight or gay, religious or atheist, Democrat or Republican, right or left. It simply is.

Today, I will make note of the beauty in the world and its unifying effect.

33

Don't Misuse Heritage

We are all the aggregate of our different origins moving through time. One is not, however, better than or greater than another. Heritage is not a badge to use to divide us from those we feel superior to, but a point of loving comparison. I can appreciate your past, and you can understand mine. After all, it is the present that we have control over. It has the most potential for good.

Today, I will allow my heritage to be a tie that binds and not a blade that divides.

Take My Hand and Follow Me

We all have wisdom. Its test, however, is the extent to which we allow it to guide our actions and help others. Amid a confusing world, our wise minds have the most value when we seek to provide a way out of darkness. Giving others the benefit of our knowledge and forethought is the highest and best use of our consciousness.

Today, I will work to extend my hand to help others along the road and allow them to benefit from my life.

The Great Experiment

Our American democracy is the test of self-determination that our country has undertaken since its inception. It juxtaposes the will of the state against the will of the people and works to allow the people to win. It embodies empowerment in its purest form, which is the ability of each of us to live our lives to the fullest and help others to do the same. Its language has been co-opted in recent times to represent fringe views that do not reflect the overall will. The phrase "We the People" doesn't belong to any one group that claims to have a corner on true patriotism. Instead, it is a symbol of the all-inclusive purpose of our freedom itself in the context of raising all boats. It includes participants of every gender identity, race, class, sexuality, and level of ability.

Today, I will support the true spirit of the American Experiment.

Be a Servant

Mastery of others speaks to the lust for power. It is selfish and, by definition, divisive, as it seeks to define a power differential and tries to order society on that basis. Being a servant leader, however, supports the whole. It binds us together, honoring the common good over the achievements of the few. It allows us to truly see others for what they are in their state of need. It will enable us to stand together on common ground.

Today, I will seek to serve and not overpower.

Dismantle an Obstacle Today

The walls between us were not built in a moment but grew organically out of years of misunderstanding, injustice, and ignorance. Their height was not preordained but developed out of the sum of each of us looking away instead of facing each other to tend to mutual needs. The walls were built like that, but they can be torn down in the same incremental way.

Today, I will seek to remove at least one personal obstacle between me and a genuine understanding of others.

Tell Me Why That Is

Other people don't always bother to demonstrate their motives. They may be rooted in misunderstanding or in the sort of hatred that has been passed from generation to generation. We are left to construe our own meaning. This tends to be inaccurate, as we cannot be both the sum of their experiences and the sum of our own. Communication promotes understanding. Simply ask others about their motivations.

Today, I will be mindful of asking other people reasons for their actions before I react.

Releasing Hatred

Old wounds are divisive. Hatred and distrust are the poisons that push us apart and prevent consensus. Even though our resentments may be justified, they are counterproductive. They keep us from realizing our full potential as a unified whole. We must approach this with a peaceful tongue and make amends where necessary.

Today, I will seek to heal the damage of the past and move forward.

Healing

Polarization infects our society. Our default oppositional mindset creates a disorder of structure and function that can be hard to see past. It divides us and pushes us toward a bitter end. Unity of thought, however, can be the antidote. We do not have to succumb. Instead, we can flourish and overcome when we think and act together.

Today, I will seek to provide relief and strength to others.

41

Can I Touch the Sacred Cow?

Heroes, idols, and icons have their power because we grant it to them. In these days of division, they pass without scrutiny, and we digest them as matters of fact. To return to the middle ground, all our protected interests must be on the table. It is only in this way that we can make real, collaborative change.

Today, I will be open to relinquishing my predetermined ideals for the greater good.

Mother Earth in Red and Blue

The simple fact of science is that our planet's climate is changing at the hands of humankind. It can be empirically proven and is also evident to the naked eye in the form of extreme weather patterns. There is no hoax involved in this; nothing is gained by denial. Likely future priorities make agreement crucial. We must drop our polarity and wrap Mother Earth in both Republican red and Democratic blue and encourage unity of purpose in other countries before we pass the point of no return.

Today, I will accept the science of a changing planet and work toward our unity within it.

Reach a Little Higher

Our society's aspirations are best served when we are each aware of our abilities and how they can be expanded. This growth can contribute to a collaborative effort for mutual benefit. The surest antidote to hopelessness is the hope generated by those moving toward worthy goals. It can create momentum and become contagious.

Today, I will make every effort to broaden and contribute.

Work to Pull Extremes Back to the Center

An old friend used to say, "One thing about being out on a limb, it ain't crowded!" The crowd has found the end of the limb, however, in the form of oppositional rhetoric set in stone. The weight of extremism threatens the individual branches and the whole tree. A return to the middle ground requires that we move outlying views on both sides back to the center to save its integrity.

Today, I will work to unify bipolar viewpoints.

45

Deliver Faith from Doubt

Faith and doubt are opposites. As we hope for a solid middle ground, we must diminish the doubt about the hearts and motives of others that would keep us from trying. If we allow ourselves to trust, faith can fill areas of uncertainty. This faith does not have to be blind, but it must close its eyes to cynicism that prevents movement forward.

Today, I will work to provide faith in the face of the fearful and unknown.

Turn Toward the Good in Others

A client in my counseling practice is a computer programmer. This work requires undiluted certainty, as it "all breaks down to ones and zeros" in that world. The non-programmed world, however, has many "point five" situations that don't fit so neatly. Black-and-white thinking dictates binary choices. We must leave it behind to look for a middle ground and see the positives in others. We must seek it and lean into it!

Today, I will avoid polarized thinking and merely look for the good in others.

Sincerity

Polarization leaves us not knowing which side to trust. Truth gets diluted by too many agendas, greed, and power. The integrity of an individual's word can become suspect and lead us to make snap judgments. Do they say what they mean? A return to the middle dictates that we do our best to offer earnest and genuine thoughts and discourse, even if we are the only ones doing so.

Today, I will try to put my true self forward.

Release God from Your Captivity

No one has dominion over a Higher Power. The concept is not a part of anyone's branding or suppositions but lives its own immutable identity. Its arms are stretched wide, encompassing both the poles of our society. Right and wrong can thus remain relative, fitting each of us as a function of our understanding. No one group can define them entirely or claim ownership. Instead, coexistence offers peace and unity.

Today, I will let go of any idea that I have a monopoly on thoughts of right and wrong.

On the Path to Peace

The path to peace may be difficult. There may be obstacles in the way, old habits to break, and old thoughts to eliminate. It is more of an attitude than specific steps. If we remain open to commonality, it becomes more of a possibility over time. It is something that we can all enjoy as a collaborative truth.

Today, I will do my best to have my actions lead to peace.

What People Say When They Are Hurting

There are not many of us who haven't wished we could take back things that we have said. The heat of the moment produces its own temperature and becomes the territory of misplaced passions. In today's politics, passions run high, and people verbalize their wounds. The middle ground then becomes a place of forgiveness and hope, where we account for this but still take the other person on the whole of their existence.

Today, I will be mindful of forgiving those around me for saying the wrong thing.

51

We All Need a Home Together

Although we all got here differently, each of us has become a part of the American story. Our roots are planted here. This is true whether we chose this country as a home, were brought here, or were born here. It is our responsibility to provide everyone with the same fertile ground. The path forward recognizes that this is an immutable truth.

Today, I will understand that others are entitled to their place alongside me on the path to the common good.

Restore Faith in Elections

Sinister thoughts run rampant in the context of election results not being in a particular candidate's favor. We cannot believe that they have lost, even in the face of contrary facts. Instead of gracefully accepting the choice of the voters, we look for ways to undermine the system at its roots instead of internalizing the fairness of its outcomes. This is a reach for power at its most basic level. Removing this dynamic requires thoughtfulness and objectivity. The middle ground requires the absence of bias or prejudice.

Today, I will affirm my faith in our democratic process.

53

Haven't We Done This Before?

Much of the political divide today lives in familiar territory. Our nation has endured many fractious times, from the Civil War forward through the civil rights movement to war protests. While the drama of the present moment gives fuel to the thought that our democracy may fail, the middle ground helps us give way to the idea that we have been in situations of discord before and that our institutions have prevailed. This is a function of the will of our citizens to give democracy its legitimacy and foundation.

Today, I will work to normalize some degree of division in others' minds while maintaining the whole.

Just Like Me

The rhetorical climate in our society leaves us standing at opposite poles. We can't conceive of coming to a middle ground that looks a bit like all of us. This concept, however, exists intrinsically. We have more commonality physically, emotionally, and spiritually than we are even aware of. We can find solid footing.

Today, I will work to join opposing sides as one beautiful whole.

Not Just Today

Our walk toward unity cannot be a part-time endeavor. Divisions have been driven so far into our society, and they were not placed there overnight. It will take a sustained effort to bring our discourse back to common courtesy. It was not removed in a brief time, so it will take a long-term effort to get it back.

Today, I will commit to perseverance and putting forth the effort to unify over the long term.

Simple Respect

Even within conflict, there is a need for both form and substance. While we may be irrevocably convinced that we have the right answer, it is important to honor those with whom we disagree. Polarization may make this feel like a lost art, but it is the gentle avenue down which true solutions move.

Today, I will understand the value of universal respect.

Tearing Down Walls at Work

Most of us spend a great deal of time at work with others, whether in person or through the internet. While it is a familiar environment, it is not always a place where deep knowledge of others or deep commitment takes place. The offhand comment or seemingly benign action on the part of others can place them in a pigeonhole, and we seldom take the time to remove them from it. People with opinions opposed to our own wind up firmly in the "they" column. While the workplace is also not a consistently good place to work out emotions, we can still bring mindfulness to bear. A word of understanding or compassion in action may help us get to a middle ground with others where none exists. This seems crucial as we attempt to formalize facing inward in our society to meet common goals.

Today, I will strive to extend my hand to others in my workplace with sincerity.

Living with Atrocity

Deep division and a lack of concern for others bring about an atmosphere where hatred and atrocity can fill the void. Heinous actions can seem justified by some as the only available alternatives. These must be seen for what they are. They are outliers. They are not solutions.

Today, I will not automatically hold wrongs against entire groups. I will seek to fix accountability narrowly.

59

Suit Up and Show Up

Reaching out to others to invite them to the middle ground is not always successful. At times, it truly is the fault of others for not responding to our overtures. In these instances, it becomes more about keeping our side of the street clean. Attempting to meet in the middle requires us to only "suit up and show up" and try to do the next correct thing in each situation. Even if each interaction does not meet in the middle, we can be hopeful that the sum of sincere efforts will sway the minds of others.

Today, I will be mindful that I can only attempt to bring people to the middle.

Immediate Problems

Discord in our society must be met with urgency. Factual disagreements over what will likely prove to be irrefutable science or the final results of demagoguery and opportunism keep us apart. We have only a limited time to act. It is not imperative that we completely change everyone's minds at once. Still, we must be about the business of changing singular minds consistently to achieve change overall and preserve the common good before the opportunity to do so is gone.

Today, I will honor facts and seek to understand the urgency of bringing people to the middle ground.

61

Seek Deeper Knowledge

A more complete knowledge best serves our desire for unity. This thought applies to knowledge of circumstance, knowledge of the minds of others, and knowing that we are attempting to do the next right thing. It is the best support for decision-making that lifts us all higher. We must seek it with thirst and hunger.

Today, I will seek to surround myself with truthful information.

Emotions Are Not Always Facts

The emotional nature of our divided society lends itself to irrational and untrue opinions of the other side. We disparage others and shoot from the hip when unnecessarily. We seemingly refuse to look beneath the surface. Unity calls on us to be more intentional in our dealings with people and situations.

Today, I will seek to apply logic instead of blind passion to my interactions.

Consistency

Our desire to create a new middle ground cannot be a casual endeavor. We cannot evoke reconciliation only when it suits us or only when it furthers a selfish goal. To bring about true societal change, each divisive thought must be met with a new inclusive thought every time possible. We must be even and steady in our pursuit of the hearts and minds of others.

Today, I will take consistent action to invite others to unity.

We Author the New Normal

Polarization has been the norm for so long that it feels as though we are grieving unified thought as a lost cause. This cannot be the case. We must strive to create a new normal ground of unity. It will not consist of old ideas from the past but will strive to put items into place that are of utility to everyone going forward. This is a difficult task but a worthy one.

Today, I will note aspects of the unity I am building that are new but can become routine and habituated.

It Takes a Step Back to Us

It is easy to get discouraged as we attempt to bring others to a middle ground. This path is full of incremental challenges and success, as well as backward steps and failure. We must believe, however, that solutions will take a step back toward us if we take a step toward them. The sum of these tiny solutions can eventually equal a whole that floats all boats.

Today, I will resolve to take a step forward regardless of the results. I will trust that I am adding to the greater good.

A Baseline of Love

In seeking unity, we must build a firm ground that is built on the foundation of love for one another. Love does not equal complete agreement but rather an understanding of the rights of others to their opinion if it differs from our own. We must be overt about showing others that they are still valued and loved, even in conflict. In this loving way, we put our best foot forward in nurturing a fertile place for future steps toward the middle.

Today, I will lead with love.

Simple Respect

Amid heated rhetoric, much of the art of simple humanity can get lost. People say spiteful and aggressive things. While some of these things may be rooted in verifiable truth, they should be delivered with simple humanity that takes into account the dignity of others.

Today, I will be mindful to offer those around me respect even if I disagree with them.

Speak from the Heart

Much of the time, we operate in the construct of cold empirical facts and a singularly minded attitude toward them. It is easy to forget to speak to one another from a place of sincerity. In many instances, one heartfelt sentence can do more to advance a cause or solve an issue than twelve sentences based on raw data.

Today, I will make it a point to offer sincerity first.

Lead When No One Is Watching

Consistency of purpose is necessary to implement true change. The incremental shift in thought needed to reunify us will probably not be sweeping. Foundational change may take time. Accolades will not be immediate, but the potential reward is great. We should be mindful to continue to do the next right thing in the cause of unity and let approval and acclaim take care of themselves.

Today, I will consistently seek common ground, even when it is inconvenient and not appreciated.

Love Peace

During our divisiveness, both sides seem to revel in the rancor of evil rhetoric. Conflict and division bring about chaos, and the tendency is to automatically oppose the other side without thinking. Disturbance is seen as a means to an end. A move toward unity will require espousing the healing power of peace.

Today, I will promote the love of peaceful discourse.

71

Insurrection

Extreme politics appear to give some of us license to ignore the rule of law. They are motivated to simply try to take what they want and are not willing to give back to a greater whole. This defies societal values and is the path to anarchy. A unified people must refute this in the strongest terms.

Today, I will understand that I cannot just force the change that I want in a free society.

What's in It for Us?

In a nation based on capitalism, our profit or gain in any situation is usually the first thing that comes to mind. While it is true there is no mission without money, it cannot be the only motivator. Left to its own devices, it leads to further polarization as the invisible hand works to feed itself. Instead, we should feed the whole to gain a unified result for all. If we do, we can see that altruism is not only its own reward but that it can lead us to personal reward as well.

Today, I will take steps to ensure that everyone can have a slice of a bigger pie.

73

Collapse

Although some of us have decried the evils of the status quo of a particular "current day" for generations, there is now an existential imperative to move away from our divisive path. Civil order and our very democracy are at stake. Polarized factions work to push us so far apart that we seem to be crumbling, losing the center to a degree where it is becoming harder and harder to find footing. We must change this pattern before the implosion sucks in literally everything we value. Time is of the essence as we seek to affirm a solid ground.

Today, I will honor the emergent need to make positive change.

Know Your Own Heart

The path back to real unity requires introspection. It involves thoroughly reviewing our motives in real time, moving events toward the greater good. It also requires evaluating ourselves to present outward logic that works for the whole of society. If we honor our emotional minds in this process, our actions will have the ring of sincerity and purpose.

Today, I will look within to discover a truth that I can share.

75

Taking Time to Listen

Our society is polarized to the point where no one tries to listen through the din for anything approaching substance anymore. We take what our side has given us and run with it without regard for other viewpoints. Only by turning the volume down on the discourse can we hear things of value from all sides.

Today, I will work to make way for opposing viewpoints and amplify them for consideration.

What Are the Things That Matter?

The world is full of extraneous situations. These have the effect of diverting us from the truth, from things that fulfill us and shape our hearts. More than this, the random nature of chaos presents a thousand rabbit trails that invite us to turn away from others and widen gaps. The rewards for focusing past this are a more genuine heart and sharper senses. They have the power to define us and bring us together.

Today, I will seek to look beyond the headline.

77

Be Welcoming

Intransigence can leave us with a narrow understanding of what the next steps toward unity might look like. We must break apart things we have set in stone and be open to new concepts and actions that may impact the greater good. Arms held wide open bring hope for a sustainable middle ground with the broadest base possible.

Today, I will seek to be more inclusive both in thought and action.

The Information Jungle

Modern existence is a deluge of information and an avalanche of viewpoints. It has increasingly become the job of the media to titillate and entertain rather than to seek truth. The path back to a livable middle ground requires us to look behind a headline and verify for ourselves the integrity of its statement. It will require us to weigh opinions and turn away from demagoguery objectively.

Today, I will consider the source as I digest media.

Turn Off the Gaslight

Feedback from our divided society can defy common sense. It can fly in the face of reason, telling us that even the things we can verify are not going on. Those who seek to manipulate us try to wear us down. They count on our inability to check facts. It is our responsibility as citizens to continue to hold fast regardless of what others might say in order to cloud our understanding.

Today, I will work to promote verifiable truth and to marginalize those who would refute it.

Build a Foundation

The return to common ground requires a central desire for cooperation. While problems are not usually solved in a day, each resolved difficulty allows us to put one more brick in place upon which a structure of solidarity can be built. We must be incremental in laying the groundwork for a truly functional and inclusive society.

Today, I will seek to understand that today's actions underlie tomorrow's successes.

81

Restore Civility

Rancorous discourse prevails in our culture. Our behavior and speech are so far from formal politeness and regard for others that the word civility has all but left our vocabulary. The right and the left routinely disparage each other, pushing the poles farther apart. This act leaves the middle ground so thin that it doesn't seem to support what was once taken for granted in our society. Unity demands our concerted effort to rebuild love, or at least positive regard.

Today, I will be mindful of my words and deeds and work to reinforce accommodation without insult.

What Am I Adding Today?

Expanding the middle ground requires us to question what we might be tearing down and our willingness to work to build things up. Adding our time, intent, and skill for the good of all elevates the center. Our helping hand of assistance serves as an invitation to others and an endowment of greater things for the generations behind us. It supplies the building blocks for a non-polarized society.

Today, I will seek to increase the sum of good works.

83

Seek Collective Wisdom

Good outcomes are the sum of the wise decisions made to bring them about. We are at our best when we use our savvy and intellect collaboratively. In this way, achievements gain the strength of consensus and the confidence that we have brought our best minds to bear. This is foundational as we build a more thoughtful society. We can actively seek best practices regardless of affiliations or personal credit.

Today, I will work to offer my best to others to bring about wisdom.

Recognize a Lying Voice

An objective search for the truth must be the underlying foundation of our search for a workable middle ground. We cannot take the declarations of others with something to gain as gospel truth without thinking for ourselves. We must hold each of these voices up to a defining light. While demagogues seek to marginalize those in their way, we must seek to expose lies and marginalize them instead.

Today, I will do my part to bring the truth to an unbiased light.

What Can I Do to Make It Right?

Society's broad divisions leave in their wake injustice, inequality, and outrage. Our polarized discourse and deeds litter the middle ground with hurt and shame. The only way to reinforce unity that works is to recognize our part in the wrongs of the past and ask what we can do in this moment to advance atonement. Today's amends are the foundation of tomorrow's unity.

Today, I will seek to understand my part in the past and my contribution to the future.

A Little More Mr. Nice Guy

We live in a contentious society with more powerful public disagreement than ever before. Closed minds draw lines in the sand, and insult is the order of the day. The sheer force of conviction pushes us apart without consideration. Finding our way back to solidarity will require a gentler approach that seeks to curb defensiveness and allow cooperation.

Today, I will work to bring civility and dignity to my discourse with others.

A Single Act of Forgiveness

Divided political discourse has not only driven a wedge between us and others at large, but it has also separated good friends and caused rifts in close relationships. Differences of opinion, no matter how sincere, should not be allowed to break the ties that bind. Divergent opinions do not warrant a loss of respect or isolation. We are stronger together.

Today, I will try to say the first kind word and reach across to mend differences.

Remove This from Me

Acrimony and animosity held inward turn into resentment. It has the unfortunate power to pick us up and carry us away. Even if we approach our resentments with a logical mind, our emotional mind can still harbor ounces of venom that we can't reason away. In whatever way we find it, spirituality can be a place to deposit these slivers of bitterness and allow them to fade. It may be the only way we can get some of these outside of ourselves.

Today, I will ask a power greater than myself to remove resentment.

They Aren't All Stupid

Too often, our knee-jerk defense of a point of view is to demean the intellect of the other side. It is shallow at its best and perhaps dangerous at its worst. Intelligent people can disagree. We are all the sum of our own experiences, and the fact that someone else's journey has led to an opposite conclusion may be inevitable based on circumstance. Unity insists that we at least make an effort to understand each other's thoughts and what brought them about.

Today, I will be mindful of the intellect of others regardless of how much I disagree with them.

Picking a Side

Our divided discourse seems to insist that we choose one side or the other. While we are denying our humanity if we don't seek to align with people of shared values, the move to unity insists that this need to choose and a heart open to inclusiveness are not mutually exclusive. We can be who we are and still work to be unbiased and understanding.

Today, I will be true to myself and my beliefs while still holding space for others.

Hold Yourself Open

Our divided world is a confusing place. Conflicts leave us at the edge of our intellect, and our weary hearts can see no peace available. Empathy allows us to be open to the path of unity, opening our arms to others. Perhaps we will be the light of reason where none exists or the inspiration when the facts dictate doom.

Today, I will be mindful to hold my arms outstretched to encourage others.

We Must Assemble the Rainbow

Active love must be the building block for the kind of national discourse that encourages us all to reach for something higher together rather than a separate half-truth. There must be room in our hearts for the consciousness of others and a firm hand toward achieving a new society that allows us to flourish together. This sensibility can work to make waiting out the storm of alienation worth it.

Today, I will understand that it takes all colors of existence to create a rainbow that shines.

When My Honor and Yours Differ

Interpretations of morality, integrity, and ethics differ between people. Standards of honorable behavior are not universal. They vary depending on our experiences in society, religion, and situations. They should not be imposed on others as the only path. Unity asks us to look beyond our definitions and consider the convictions of others without judgment.

Today, I will seek to understand others in the context of what is right for each of us as individuals.

Take Off the War Paint

Our division begins with adversarial relationships. First impressions are lasting, and it is difficult to find a middle ground after we have radiated conflict and a lack of empathy when we first encounter people. An open countenance can put us on the road to unity before relationships start.

Today, I will be mindful of my presentation to others.

Release Fear of the Future

Facts dictate that we keep one eye toward the future to lead orderly lives. Despite this, the difference that we need to make in favor of unity also dictates that we live in the present moment. Doing the work of coming back together in the here and now is our only method of building toward a future that includes all of us. We must do this work to the fullness of our capacity. If we do, the future will take care of itself.

Today, I will stay in the here and now and offer my efforts to peace and solidarity.

Rewriting the Playbook to Include Others

An inclusive society invites the full participation of all. To achieve agreement, we must consider the thoughts and interests of others whose views diverge from our own as we make plans. The presence of opposing viewpoints will not evaporate just because we shut our eyes to them. Extremism only builds a more divided house.

Today, I will incorporate opinions that differ from my own as I seek to build society.

Lose the Battle Cries

Heightened emotions make it easy to just go with the inertia of the moment. Our urges to act on these feelings seem to be endlessly supplied with catchphrases that berate and damn our adversaries. Working towards the middle ground requires us to apply more thought. If we pause when agitated with the other side, we can allow room for dialogue that rises above fighting words and reaches for peaceful solutions.

Today, I will seek to deepen discourse and not merely parrot the talk of the day.

How Can I Help You?

A good neighbor once told me that he felt that we were put here on this Earth to help one another. His attitude of service resonated with me for several days, even though I am pretty sure he is on the other side of the political spectrum from me. Service allows us to listen, love, and forgive others. Its focus brings us closer to the kind of unity which makes us all stronger.

Today, I will seek to be of maximum service.

Step One Together

The journey back to unity must begin with an initial action. The nature of this first step is not always evident. If we are intentional about seeking it, however, we can usually discover a clear path forward that includes others. It is the act of taking the step, not the result, which is significant.

Today, I will seek to find a beginning mutual step toward harmony.

Less My Way or the Highway

Our rigid positions and stereotypes perpetuate themselves. Pride can take over when logic offers a better way. Even if we believe there are points of non-negotiation and absolutes, we should examine each situation in context and be honest with ourselves as to whether they apply. A lack of accommodation can be the enemy of practical solutions.

Today, I will keep my mind open to solutions that defeat intransigent tendencies that do not serve me well.

Amends

The fact that we cannot change the past is an intractable truth. Our past actions or those of others in our group cannot be undone. However, it is possible to remove past wrongs as obstacles. A sincere effort to make amends can place us in a position to author a new truth with those around us.

Today, I will seek to offer redress to soften the sting of past transgressions and find new common ground.

Be the Light in the Room

Brilliance attracts. Actions that we have held up to the light gain the commonality of spirit and resonate across differences. While there are many concepts of truth, we can seek not to parse out differences but rather create a new ethos where we can all aspire to better things.

Today, I will seek to illuminate the darkness and provide new directions.

Call Them by Their Names

Today's vitriolic landscape leads us to hold others in contempt. We highlight our differences with dark generalization. We encapsulate the perceived "other side" in short jabs of language which make us feel as though we have gone back to junior high school. Unity insists that we make an effort to simply refer to others as they want to be referred to despite our opinion of their thoughts, actions, or motives.

Today, I will make the extra effort to speak to others in a personal way that accurately addresses them.

I Won't Assume I Know You

We are all the product of a varied journey. Polarization tells us that we know in exact terms what is in the minds of others without asking. It is presumptuous to think that this is true. If we look at the history understand their origins. We then have a chance to learn the heart of those we disagree with without making automatic judgments.

Today, I will endeavor to get to know others without relying solely on perception.

All Are Welcome

Our division perpetuates the exclusivity of our groups. We exclude people by labels rather than understanding everyone on their merits. A strong movement towards harmony dictates that we open our arms wide. This action melts away the walls of the past, allowing us to come together physically and spiritually.

Today, I will do my best to be inclusive and invite the input and presence of all.

Honesty

Deception is at the core of division. It pushes us to accept thoughts that are fed to us rather than embrace our intellect. We often internalize group speak and echo it without regard for the truth. Unity expects us to be objective and not allow the fidelity of thoughts and actions to be covered up by mob mentality. We must not seek to manipulate but rather to enlighten.

Today, I will seek to be truthful in both thoughts and actions.

Live and Let Live

Disagreement does not demand that we vanquish those who do not share our opinions. We can famously "agree to disagree" without any undue proselytizing insistence that others be in lockstep with us. Accommodation and diversity move us closer to a common identity that is all-encompassing and moves the whole forward.

Today, I will seek not to vilify or destroy but rather build up and encourage.

Work to Shape the Future

Our current divisions leave a gap that never closes if we do not apply effort. If we become laissez-faire and do not lead in this way, things tend to grow wild and apart. We must seek direct action to shape coming events in a way that fosters interconnection.

Today, I will do my best to guide others in the moment toward a common good.

Take Mine

Selflessness is a lost art. Self-seeking motives push us toward getting more than we are giving. A growing heart, however, prompts us to offer ourselves to others. In this way, we can gain unity in its most palpable sense. We must give of ourselves to supply the raw materials that create a society capable of caring for all in sufficient measure.

Today, I will seek to give rather than to receive.

No More Moral Injury

Our current divisive society tends to override our sense of morality to categorize people and promote evil. We identify too much with groups that insist on principles that fly in the face of the deepest parts of our nature and ideas of right and wrong. Conscience demands that we make our own choices about the rectitude of actions. We must move away from precepts and toward unity and empathy. We are called upon to reach for this truth within circumstances and act based upon it.

Today, I will not allow crowd ethos to dictate my ethics.

My Mistake

Consensus demands that we examine our behavior. Our actions must be compared to a standard that considers a unified goal rather than a fractious one. We must take ownership of our errors. While not demonizing ourselves, we apply thoughts of equity and admit when we are wrong.

Today, I will take responsibility for my actions and examine them in the context of others and their needs.

The Evil of Bad Memory

Old wounds are easy to open. Even after redress, some wrongs are held close to the heart by their very nature. They can cloud judgment and become a virus that infects the present with the poison of the past. Unity does not hold grudges but seeks to repeatedly hold new beginnings more closely.

Today, I will turn away from the bad of the past and toward the good of the present.

The Empowerment Factor

Our divided society fails to empower those who would reconcile divisions. True forward movement dictates more than lip service. It asks for a genuine sharing of intelligence, time, and resources to reach a common goal. They must have the necessary tools.

Today, I will work to allocate resources that move us toward unity.

Respect Sacrifice

The surest way to common ground is to honor and revere the efforts of others. Even if their work is misdirected in our eyes, their deeds are generally the product of sincere feelings. They often come from others' individual concepts of duty and integrity, no matter how skewed those might be. Building commonality reveres all work as the product of the fidelity of those who offer it. This paves the path forward.

Today, I will recognize what others have done in the past as we look toward a unified future.

Help Me Understand You

We are all shaped on separate paths. Mine may have varied from yours, and the extremes of this variance push us further apart. I cannot walk your walk. Moving toward common ground dictates that I ask you for clarity as I search for your motives and seek to reconcile them.

Today, I will seek knowledge instead of allowing misunderstanding to grip me.

Close the Door on the House Divided

The hope of removing division invites us to live with intention as we seek to shut out forces that polarize us. We must pull these emotional mind extremes away from our hearts and allow a clean break to a new day. Building a new house demands that we leave the old one behind.

Today, I will seek to behave in a way that leaves inequity and sadness in the past.

The Power of Just One Moment

Experience can be altered by one brief, powerful new state of being that radiates peace. These are the direct building blocks of the future. Standing together encourages us to incorporate these as we move forward and allow the good to permeate. They become the measure of the past and inform the future.

Today, I will seek to identify essential moments and acknowledge them.

Behaving like the Last Day

Repairing the past and informing unity involves a sense of urgency. We are not guaranteed tomorrow. Even if it exists, the future that we hope to go to together may not look like an acceptable destination unless we can dedicate ourselves to outcomes in the present moment.

Today, I will honor the pressing need for unity and act promptly.

Try for Something Deeper

So much of our divisive rhetoric is reflexive. We have picked sides and automatically disagree when the other side mentions an item or presents an issue. This impulse makes it challenging to find common ground in real time. However, within the nuance of issues, there may be a place where we can stand together.

Today, I will look below the first layer, seeking unity.

Is Belief Enough?

Our division has caused us to lose faith in one another. We feel hopeless, convinced that the other side is incapable of empathy. This may seem true in some instances, but a desire for peace must insist that we believe in a harmonious default and seek to find it.

Today, I will practice faith and belief.

Move the Barriers

Division generally starts with a wedge driven between us. Barriers turn the common ground into a minefield that seems too treacherous to venture into. We can find solidarity only if we work to remove obstacles in good faith. The removal of the wedge starts with us.

Today, I will seek to remove stumbling blocks to communication instead of placing them in the way.

The Good Old Days

We tend to venerate only our version of the past, pointing to what is wrong with the present and longing for what was theoretically a "simpler time" that was better. We use this vision of the past to justify our polarization in the present. We convince ourselves that the other side and their versions of the "good past" are somehow wrong and not valid. While we are all products of the past, moving to the middle dictates that we work to make the present better and more cooperative.

Today, I will seek to make today better and less divisive instead of leaning on the past.

Be Willing to Comfort

Loss is as inevitable as aging and dying. It is universal. Discounting the losses of other people is divisive and denies their humanity. Conversely, honoring the losses of others reaches across the chasm and fosters unity.

Today, I will work to recognize the humanity in others and their feelings at times of loss regardless of which side they are on.

Take Them with You

Leading toward unity involves looking into the eyes of others, taking them by the hand, and walking with them. Placing hostility and division aside, we can search for something that resonates. Both sides must be present to find common ground.

Today, I will endeavor to walk with those who disagree with me toward the unification of spirit.

Qualified Acceptance

The thought of love may be a bridge too far regarding those that we disagree with strongly. Unanimity does not insist that we totally disregard the bad motives of others but rather that we find those parts that we can at least tolerate for the common good. In this way, we can remain separate human beings of conscience but still advance alliances.

Today, I will understand that I do not have to love the totality of others, but I commit to the search for aspects that bind us together.

Accepting Sadness

Division has led our society to heinous acts, anguish, and bitterness. It is naïve to think that the evil acts of the past will not cause us pain. The only reasonable result, however, must be the desire to improve circumstances so that the destructive behavior does not have to be repeated.

Today, I will understand that the road forward includes past suffering but continues to look ahead toward better days.

Dysfunctional Government

The experiment of our democracy is at an impasse as our evenly divided society attempts to make rules. Individual thought gives way to party identity and self-interest. This can only change when we demand that our representatives regard the collective interest first and make decisions based on logic. This is not an unattainable goal.

Today, I will be mindful of my ability to speak truth to power.

Say Goodbye to Dogma

Many of the world's religions demand a proselytizing heart. We are sent forward with a vision of a Higher Power that demands that everyone believe just as we do. It is impossible to move together if we refuse to see the faith of others and accept it at face value. If we do, we have a chance to move toward faith's best unified result. From a higher ground, we can leave interpretation to individuals.

Today, I will understand that my beliefs are not the only path to the greater good.

We Are All in This Together

We are not all that far apart. Common worries like economic security and personal safety bind us together as we seek solutions. Universal desires give us commonality and can serve to blunt our differences. The resulting middle ground makes it easier for everyone to achieve them. We must work with willing hands and a loving heart, seeking to maximize the degree to which everyone's needs are met.

Today, I will do my best to recognize common bonds and value them.

Can We All Be Patriots?

There is a difference between patriotism and nationalism. Nationalism embodies division because it considers only some people worthy. Patriotism, however, allows all of us to come from divergent viewpoints to love our country and create a better one.

Today, I will understand that being a true patriot involves bringing everyone to the table and moving forward.

The Fear Factor

It is easy to be afraid of what we do not understand. We look at evidence from the past and draw a line between bad previous outcomes and the current situation. The road to unity asks us to put aside our fears to achieve stronger bonds. This path can work to remove anxiety from the future and move others to action.

Today, I will lead by inspiration.

Speak Outside the Echo Chamber

Truth requires us to look outside the lines to get to the true heart of issues. Listening only to the viewpoints of others that match ours is comforting, and the feedback we get from them feels like safety in numbers. If we allow them to, the opinions of those who disagree with us can expand our understanding and possibly lead to better solutions.

Today, I will be mindful to listen to opposing views.

The Dog Whistle

Division among us motivates some to disguise their true motives in ways that are intended to dilute the sting of prejudice. Even when it is minimized, it still exists. It is the poison that pits us against one another. True unity must contain an overt embrace instead of a covert attack.

Today, I will consistently push back against unspoken bias.

Disagreeing More Effectively

The simple act of disagreeing brings about division. The depth of this division is dependent upon what aspect of the dispute we place our energy behind. Contempt, if given fuel, pushes us to opposite ends. Polarization decreases when we genuinely consider opposing viewpoints and offer verifiable facts to the other side. A middle ground is built upon a common, deep understanding after investigation.

Today, I will turn away from disrespect and offer reason instead.

Standing for Something

Is it possible to stand for something and be flexible? Underlying principles guide actions. If we try to see the truth in situations beneath the surface, we can understand how others came to their conclusions. We can turn discourse toward the common possibility of love and unity. This is based on common aspects of character that we can all believe in.

Today, I will defend my beliefs in a way that allows others to find a path to agree with me on basic principles.

Release Snapback Cynicism

Doubting the sincerity of others becomes a harmful habit. It is easier to dismiss skeptically than to be open and thoughtful. Trusting others is not naïve. Unity asks us to continue to believe that even guarded faith in others can be rewarded.

Today, I will be careful not to judge the motives of others automatically.

We Don't Have to Follow Our Roots

Recent years have accentuated differences in our political beliefs that have become generational. There is a tendency to follow the past mindlessly, expecting a different result. Old motives leave us stuck, but the search for peace requires us to examine past motives and look for a new way forward.

Today, I will seek to illuminate the grievances of the past and seek a better future.

History That Hurts

Prejudice and intolerance find their way into our society masked as legacy. They carry on as unfortunate ill traditions and representations of hatred. We cannot allow ourselves to become helpless carriers of these past divisions and must work to create a new narrative that does not make room for the evil ghosts of the past. Unity insists that we work in the inclusive, present tense.

Today, I will be honest about history and recognize a new way forward.

Deal with the Impatience of Others

Our divided society did not reach the point of polar opposition overnight. Years of unresolved wrongs bring people to the outer edges of their forbearance, making it easy to lash out. Instead of being destructive, however, singular love insists that we make incremental progress. The totality of these steps equals better equity and a firmer foundation.

Today, I will practice self-restraint even when I am impatient for a solution.

A Firm Footing

The way forward is best defined by inclusive positions supported by detailed logic and controlled emotion. They are worthy of our confidence. We can use these as stepping stones toward a mutual understanding that moves everyone forward. Detailing this path requires our best and most sincere thought.

Today, I will be mindful to do the foundational work necessary to advance a less polarized society.

Let Them Go

Some people get so entrenched in polarization that no amount of reason can penetrate their views. While unity demands an attempt to bring them to the middle, some refuse to meet us there. Inclusion asks us not to quickly write others off as soulless "lost causes." After sincere effort with some people, however, it may be evident that our efforts are better spent elsewhere.

Today, I will try to understand that I cannot expect everyone to see value in my point of view.

Healthy Relationships with the Media

The character of our news media has changed drastically. Traditionally trusted sources seem to have given way to polarized replacements that value partisanship over truth. A thoughtful journey toward unity starts with verifiable, neutral information. In its light, we can find a way to make astute choices that benefit everyone free of affiliation or bias.

Today, I will seek to wisely control the source and volume of the media I consume.

Symbols of Unity

Symbols that we have long held as the common property of all Americans have been appropriated by different sides in possessive ways. The American flag, for example, now seems to have a religious nationalist connotation beyond its simple message of freedom for all. Common purpose demands that these symbols remain the property of the hearts of all of us. They should not be allowed to take on special meaning as a divisive rhetorical device for just a few.

Today, I will seek to honor the symbols of freedom without assuming individual ownership.

Why Must We Judge?

There is a difference between judgment and discernment. We may see a direct course of action based on facts, and we can resolve to follow it without allowing discrimination based on other factors. We must be wary of and seek to eliminate implicit bias. In this way, we can advance to a middle ground that does not condemn but rather uplifts.

Today, I will seek to be non-judgmental and work to understand instead.

I Feel Surrounded

The sheer volume of information we receive is astounding. It is easy to feel overwhelmed and isolated. In the search for unity, it is our job to understand that like-minded people remain out there despite what may seem like an inadequate small voice. If we only remember to seek, we may discover that the accord of others is closer than we think and can speak loudly.

Today, I will seek to remind myself that I am not alone and that bridges are available to the hearts and minds of others.

Real Spirituality

Polarization in our society emphasizes what seem to be diametrically opposing versions of wisdom and truth. While these are important aspects of spirituality, love and compassion are equally important. Honoring the middle ground requires both. It can guide us to a unified future.

Today, I will seek to understand the illogical by applying my heart to problems first.

Abandon Contempt

Scorn and disdain for viewpoints different from our own lead to disparagement and a lack of respect. All good relationships are built on a foundation of mutual regard. Any hope of achieving equilibrium must be predicated upon this. We must implement it through thought, action, and deed.

Today, I will react to the thoughts and beliefs of others with empathy and honor.

Find a Brother

Our ability to reach across barriers can become a skill that is honed by useful interactions with one person at a time. Even though it feels as though society as a whole cannot be changed by our small steps, finding common ground with one individual of opposing viewpoints that we can relate to is a beginning. Common ground may not be a compromise of position but rather an acknowledgment of universal human truths. Their recognition can become a path to strength and unity.

Today, I will seek a kindred spirit and mindfully prepare a place where they are willing to meet me.

Try to Notice

Awareness is the key to finding a middle ground and room to compromise. We can look for openings in others' words and facial expressions that might show us how to work with them for the common good. These prompts may not always be present, but if they are, they should never be ignored.

Today, I will view interactions through the lens of my search for unity.

Turn Your Back on the Bully

Those seeking to exploit our polarization use catchphrases and juvenile taunts to drive a deeper wedge. These appeal to our most base nature and do nothing more than add an inane static to our rhetoric. Seeking unification turns away from those hurling petty insults and toward mutual respect.

Today, I will work to marginalize those who show nothing but contempt for others.

Tearing Down the House Divided

Our oppositional discourse seems to provide the foundation for a house that is hopelessly divided. It is easy to be convinced that none of the rooms can change and that there is no basis upon which we can seek common goals. To the contrary, we are at our best when we work to dismantle this and seek to build consensus in its place. As a unified society, we can successfully and mindfully accomplish this goal.

Today, I will seek a default that tries to erase separation and embraces unity.

Selfless Sacrifice

Self-seeking motives and self-interest push us further apart. A practical middle ground requires us to give of ourselves tangibly. In this context, others can see our unifying actions and come to understand that they are stronger than divisive words. Changing actions foster changing hearts.

Today, I will promote selflessness for the common good.

Blind Allegiance

Autonomy requires each of us to think for ourselves. Regardless of the drumbeat in the background or the perceived power of one person, we are each individual with a singular voice. It is the essence of democracy to deliberately contemplate our country's choices for the road ahead. The intersection of our thoughts, based upon shared values, forms a firm foundation for unity.

Today, I will think for myself and not simply follow.

Quiet Activism

The theatrical nature of our politics leads people to believe that only those capable of making a big splash can make a difference. While those with means seem to have the advantage, we must all strive to influence minds and hearts. Affluence and privilege run riot can only be met with the faithful solidarity of many people incrementally moving toward a common goal.

Today, I will understand that my voice will be added to the sum of others to develop a powerful whole.

Keeping the Light On

Division seems to always show us a closed door and a darkened hallway. Inwardly, we may genuinely want to find a middle ground with others but become afraid to reach out to people that we feel won't be receptive because they seem to show no outward interest in sharing commonality. They may feel their own doubts and perceive this about us as well. Unification must be built upon improving these perceptions.

Today, I will be mindful of how others may see me as stubborn and be willing to be open in a way that begins a dialogue.

Restrain Your Emotions

When feelings of contempt or anger try to take over, our emotional mind can be a difficult place to find reconciliation. They overrule our logic and distract us from negotiated solutions and constructive work. Unity implores us to temper emotion, regulating partisan sentiment for the greater good.

Today, I will work to channel my emotions toward others in a way that builds a common path forward.

It Is Not Always Our Perception That Counts

Polarization doesn't leave room for alternatives. Our truth can differ from that of those on the other end of the spectrum and become an absolutist stumbling block to progress. Unanimity seeks consensus and promotes the whole. We can agree to advance issues without giving up our integrity.

Today, I will look for ways to forge agreements.

Symbolism

Both ends of the political spectrum have touchstones that encapsulate parts of their struggle. Some have historical significance, but some also cling to the past in unhealthy ways. A unified society must have the courage to evaluate these items and events in real time and understand which ones are truly representative and which ones only seek to divide in the current day. The path forward does not blame the other side for having manifestations of meaning; it just asks that they live in an atmosphere of respect.

Today, I will take an honest look at how I represent myself and my beliefs.

Are They Out to Get Us?

Division gives grudges their greatest support. It makes us think in shorthand, abandoning all reason and deliberative thought as we take our place among the mob. It is a mindset that ignores humanity and encourages us to leave insight into the motives of others at the door. Conversely, common ground understands that even a guarded optimism about the motives of others can lift us as a whole.

Today, I will seek to be less wary and more open to change.

Never Obstruction for Its Own Sake

We tend to throw down the gauntlet for the other side in a knee-jerk fashion. Automatic opposition becomes our default without really seeking the truth or middle ground. The common good implores us to be more thoughtful. Nothing can get done in an environment of preprogrammed hatred and malice.

Today, I will commit to creating a culture of reasoned dialogue and deliberative decisions.

Making Amends

Polarization has left us with open wounds and sad public realities that must be dealt with. Making amends is the first step toward unity. It insists that we admit when we are wrong and ask how to make it right. A sincere word or heartfelt change of actions can help us heal and grow together. They mend the public discourse.

Today, I will seek to correct wrongs and not repeat them.

The Ball from Left Field

Separation has led us to new extremes socially, culturally, and ethically. Just when we think something could never happen in our democracy, it rears its ugly head. We are shocked. These events come from the poles pushing further out from the center, exploring new and fearful territory. Harmony seeks to assimilate these episodes and address them thoughtfully. We cannot just tolerate new extremism. We are called on to accept the present just as it is and to act.

Today, I will understand extremes and face them without fear.

The Journey of a Thousand Miles

Our differences seem insurmountable. Pessimism dictates that there is no solution, no end in sight. We seek to right the harms of the past in one swing of the brush. In reality, these opposites were not put in place overnight. It will take an incremental, concerted effort to forge a middle ground freshly painted with caring and harmony. It will come, one brush stroke at a time.

Today, I will take my first step as an individual away from polarization and toward the common good.

Sow Love

Polarization may feel like a soulless burden that is too much for us to bear and too hard to erase. Hate is the opposite of love and a similar weight. Instead of planting discord, love demands that we offer small bits of reason to the unreasonable and make the offer of unity even to those we think we cannot abide.

Today, I will seek to show others love that might grow.

Seek a Deeper Knowledge of Kindness

Division is unkind by nature, separating us from a unified truth and a common purpose. Sometimes, positive regard is only seen in its narrowest view when we are forced to feign it as the result of circumstance. Even then, its sacrifice for a supposed cause is encouraged. Unity seeks to know kindness more intimately. It works to make it more pervasive, more practical, and more intuitive. It looks to its power to narrow gaps.

Today, I will be mindful that deeper kindness can heal differences.

A Suitcase Full of Baggage

Separation leads us down opposing paths wrought with fear and sadness. Over time, the endurance of each wrong and the echoes of shocking attacks make us wary and weary of a burden that we don't think we can shake. If allowed, our interconnection and sameness can work to remove these burdens. They can show the power of love to erase hate.

Today, I will work to lay down the hurts of the past that do not serve the common good.

Together We Rise

The trajectory of unity can carry us above hate and toward hope. It can leave the past in a place where it has less power over us and rob the future of its fear. It can provide healing, solace, and a singular vision that moves forward with the force of new beginnings.

Today, I will understand that the past can take its proper place in my heart and can be overcome by the promise of the future.

Taking Action to Change Feelings

Divisive politics leave many of us downhearted and feeling hopeless. Our thoughts join with these feelings, tending to reinforce the sadness. We don't have much control over our initial feelings, but we do have the ability to apply different thoughts and take action to change the way we feel. Moving forward indeed requires movement, initiated by the thought that something better is possible.

Today, I will look forward and act in ways that move toward a singular future.

A Truly High Tide

Our oppositional politics present many versions of economic good. Some say that enhancing those who have more will allow wealth to trickle down to those who do not. Conversely, some on the other end seek to give those less fortunate a way to rise and attain their own standards instead of simply waiting for the water to fall. Still others believe wealth is inherently evil and should not be allowed under any circumstance. Our journey to the center requires us to consider the welfare of all.

Today, I will work toward economic inclusivity that does not divide.

Respond to the Speed of Media

Polarization has grown at an alarming rate to a point where it threatens our stability. We seem to be at a crossroads, and our democracy feels as though it is imploding before we can stop it. The forces that divide us move the poles of thought to extremes with frightening momentum, complexity, and speed. This is made possible by the propaganda rushing through our super-charged information channels. This divisiveness must be met with equal force and urgency. Aggressive, savvy support for the middle ground is essential.

Today, I will respond to information onslaught and attempt to act expeditiously to bring us to unity.

Jesus as a Weapon

What once was Christianity seeking the mirror image of Jesus Christ has morphed into a form of white Christian nationalism in the minds of many. This has corrupted some believers and forced generations away from religion. It also has removed tolerance as a virtue. There is seemingly no room for doubt, dissent, or difference. It insists that Christianity equals patriotism. Our search for the middle ground must find a spiritual path forward that is inclusive and non-political.

Today, I will respect the beliefs of others and understand that the compassionate teachings of faith override politics.

Listen with Your Whole Heart

Listening is a verb. It is active, and within this action lives the seed of compromise. At its best and most useful, this activity is approached with faith and love. It is open and not judgmental. It seeks unity and allows us to present our whole heart in response if we allow it.

Today, I will commit to listening intently to others so that I can help lead them to a common spirit.

Start the Ball Rolling

Opposing sides have built walls. Between them lies a foreboding and hard-to-cross valley. It is difficult to begin change. Unity insists that just as objects that don't move stagnate, objects in motion can create inertia. Its force can move others as well.

Today, I will look for the courage to make the first push toward common ground.

Let Go of the Sad Narrative

Injustice has left us with stories that move us to tears and regret regarding the past. They masquerade as heritage and work to doom us to a future where history repeats itself. Hope and a greater commonality, however, move us to a new narrative that improves on the mistakes of the past and builds a future of peace.

Today, I will work to release the past for the good of all.

Maintain Mutual Respect

Disrespect is a poison. It moves us from faith in a middle ground to a place where opposing sides can never meet. Everyone, even an adversary, is entitled to their place in the world alongside us. Other human beings deserve our consideration, attentiveness, and regard.

Today, I will uphold principles that show decency to others.

Give Reasons

Despite our desires to face inward, there will undoubtedly be times when we cannot abandon principles to avoid conflict. Without being dogmatic, there will be points where we must be unyielding. It is our responsibility to deliver these decisions with grace and empathy in a non-dogmatic fashion. They allow dignity and respect.

Today, I will prioritize the need for explanations during times when I cannot compromise.

Leave the Labels Behind

We are far too quick to categorize people. We barely know them or don't know them at all, but we categorize, segregate, and polarize them. The path to a middle ground that works requires a fundamental shift of emphasis from the number of degrees from the center that we assign to people to the value we place upon them as a part of a central whole.

Today, I will work to look beyond the surface in my relationships with others and invite them to useful unity.

The Words We Say

Within our division, the idea of gentle discourse has been lost. We berate others with impunity, not understanding that they are human beings worthy of respect. Our words become instruments of hate and push us further apart. Unanimity requires thoughtful words that do not condemn but uplift.

Today, I will remember to elevate my words to a worthy place in service of others.

Eliminate the Tower of Babel

Current polar politics tend to speak in a language of dog whistles and echo chambers, where only members of each opposing side can understand true motives. Honesty and clarity of communication lend themselves to unity, allowing us to promote understanding for one another and move forward.

Today, I will work to use language that serves the common good and that everyone can correctly interpret.

Narrow Minds

The path away from the center started with people with small worldviews and unwillingness to compromise. Narrow-mindedness and simplistic mental summarizations of others and situations have pushed us apart. The path to alliances that work must be lined with thoughts that are outside the norm, inventive, and mindful of the welfare of all. This mindset represents true integrity.

Today, I will strive to view the thoughts of others with openness.

Misconceptions

Division draws artificial lines that seek to define character in black-and-white terms. These suppositions make no provision for misunderstanding or error and work to the destruction of peace. The middle ground is not divided by such lines but is inclusive and seeks to define others by their uniqueness and value instead of partisanship.

Today, I will seek to remove the lines that divide us.

Never Make Assumptions

Our divisive discourse becomes way too general, and we tend to draw only surface conclusions about others. Inclusivity insists that we must not base all actions upon these but rather hold an open mind and seek verification. Things are seldom what they seem, and our rich heritage is most honored when we look past assumptions to find an authentic narrative.

Today, I will not take the thoughts of others for granted as we attempt to work together.

A New View from the Top of the Mountain

It is easy to lose sight of what can be gained from a new unity of purpose. Instead of defeat for each side, it can be a victory. It can be a place where the needs of all are considered, and compromises are fashioned that make everyone stronger. It is the home of genuinely successful outcomes.

Today, I will strive to move toward a vision of a society of excellence and equity.

Absolution

Division leaves us with conflicts with others that we cannot resolve. Ideology and the desire to be right can interfere with our ability to love and empathize. Pride can also keep us from admitting when we are wrong. Peace and unity ask us to put aside differences and search for common ground. If we implement this, we are developing firm ground from which the future can take shape within compromise. It can erase estrangement.

Today, I will abandon dogmatic and absolutist thought and embrace others who have wronged me.

Old Ideas

The road to harmony is best walked in the present moment. Its path leads us to discard attitudes based on old prejudices and old ideas taken as fact without investigation. It encourages us to seek a middle ground that can be watered with empathy where none has existed before. We can then see results that continue to grow exponentially.

Today, I will discard unsound ideas from the past and replace them with forward-thinking thoughts.

Understanding the Sadness

Hopelessness surrounds our division. It is the drumbeat of resignation to the thought that there can be no common light from which we can draw inspiration. To find our way to a middle ground, we must address the hurts of others as well as our own sorrow and regret. We must be honest about it and recognize our right to our feelings while also thoughtfully moving discourse forward.

Today, I will not allow my sadness to cloud my judgment and ability to compromise.

Giving Freely

Harmony asks that we give freely and not expect specifics in return. It is the action of accommodation and the language of understanding. In discovering avenues where the opportunity to give exists, we can direct the future to return us to consensus. It becomes its own reward.

Today, I will give of myself to understand and address the views of others.

What Will Tomorrow Think of Us?

Our legacy is determined by the success or failure of the actions we take to respond to our perceptions. It is our responsibility to view our understanding in the light of genuinely universal standards of love without division. This equity will foster generational continuity and a future worth having.

Today, I will understand long-term ramifications and apply unified responses.

Keep a Brother

Learn to be loyal. True kindred spirits are hard to find. Love moves beyond the surface and is all-encompassing. Differences of opinion should not lead us to judgment of others and distance but to a desire to understand and a willingness to move closer and give grace when we cannot agree. There is a difference between love and perfect agreement, and love can transcend all.

Today, I will love first and not judge.

Don't We All Pray?

The different ways in which we approach a Higher Power have inherent division. Thoughts of having the "one true way" interfere with our ability to empathize with and understand the spiritual path of others. As we seek understanding, we must also seek unanimity and an understanding that we are taking divergent paths to the same strength.

Today, I will not seek to proselytize but to embrace the spirituality of others as we work toward a common good.

Stop the Vitriol

Our current polarized political landscape is super-charged with the most hateful rhetoric and attitudes. We vilify our supposed enemies, often letting others tell us to treat them with no mercy because they are inherently evil. Unity insists upon leadership that moves us to the center instead of fanning the flames of evil discourse.

Today, I will choose leaders that espouse dignity rather than hatred.

On Respecting Process

We have accepted specific processes to have a functional society. While respecting these can sometimes ensure directional movement, it is our job within solidarity to change processes when they are not moving in the direction of an effective result for the whole. Routines that move us toward division and away from togetherness and hope should be reevaluated within our need for unity. A lockstep is not required.

Today, I will not blindly follow convention but move through it with an open mind and heart. I will hold space for improvement.

Empathy as a Rule

The journey to the middle ground requires us to consider others' needs. We must understand their point of view and why their experiences may be different from our own. Only by fulfilling mutual needs will we be able to develop a future that carries us all forward.

Today, I will commit to developing an understanding and awareness of others to build consensus.

Be Impartial

Our partisan societal divide has left us with many prejudices. These cloud decision-making at best and completely close minds at worst. A unified future comes into focus when we are able to put aside partiality and apply equity to all situations. Only in this way can we embrace those who seem to be on the other side.

Today, I will work to take only objective actions.

Focus on the Solution

Our divisive nature surreptitiously crept up upon us over a long time. It will take mindful focus to move us to the center. Extremism and distraction threaten this progress. The bedrock of solidarity must be the thoughtful consideration of and consistent application of inclusion.

Today, I will turn aside from things that divert me from enhancing unity.

Leave Hatred Behind

Hatred is a strong emotion. It moves simple disagreement into the emotional region of irrationality, from which there is no return. Belonging to a group that professes hatred for others is not thinking through the consequences. It leaves no room for the common good and only sees red instead of the colors of the rainbow. True inclusivity demands that we identify the difference between dislike and hatred and act guided by logical thought as opposed to chaotic passion.

Today, I will commit to seeing others with a measure of love and empathy.

Normalize the Taboo

In our dire state of division, no subject can be off-limits. We must move in all directions to develop common ground. While maintaining our boundaries and personal morality, we must remain open to the discussion of difficult subjects. We must speak the unspeakable when necessary. We must deny our fear of change and have faith that hard conversations can come to fruitful ends.

Today, I will not be fearful of any subject in my quest for unity.

What Are Our Common Goals?

Although cultural division would suggest otherwise, we do have universal goals. Safety, love, sustenance, and dignity are necessary for all of us. Promoting these can become a common purpose, defeating separation and providing peace. It can be the starting point for consensus.

Today, I will consider others' goals, look for intersections with my needs, and then offer a hand of peace.

Be Inclusive

Our society was founded on ideals that have become a broad spectrum of expressions of freedom and well-being. Instead of accentuating differences, we can include others. This broad scope enhances the common good as we move toward implementing the ideas of many instead of the dictates of only a few. It allows our best chance for survival.

Today, I will open my arms wide and welcome everyone who would like to contribute.

Aren't We Tired of This?

Our differences have pushed us so far apart that trying to bridge the political and societal gap has become a seemingly impossible task. We bring weary hands to the work of unification, as we are often mentally exhausted by division itself and do not have the capacity to offer solutions to problems. It feels as though we have little to give. The collective push for unity can rise above this, as every small incremental step can add to momentum as a whole. Together, the sum of our meager abilities adds up to an undeniable force for change.

Today, I will set aside divisive words and actions and their exhaustion.

Stop Demanding Perfection

The middle ground must be a place where old hurts are disregarded for the common good. While it is difficult to forget them logically, we must work to release them emotionally and let them go to move forward. We must embrace one another's imperfect selves to build sustainability.

Today, I will resolve to release old hurts as I meet others in the middle with an understanding of their humanity.

Gridlock

Our differences lead us to a deadlock. Nothing seems to get done in the vacuum between opposing viewpoints. Our institutions are clogged with unworkable results of division. A new way forward must be based on reconciliation and compromise so that the business of our entire society can move forward in an orderly way. Opposition, for its own sake, only leads to chaos. We are better than this!

Today, I will make it a point to let decision-makers know that I want them to compromise with honor to benefit the whole.

Not Good, Not Bad, Just Different

Today's polarization leads us to vilify the other side. It is much easier to maintain our "good" decisions if we can starkly contrast them to the "bad" that others introduce. In reality, the truth almost always lies somewhere on this spectrum. Voicing our differences does not always have to be qualitative or judgmental. We can disagree and still respect the other side.

Today, I will give the opinions of others a chance to prove themselves as simply a different approach.

Find Considerate Balance

Sometimes, the common ground may only consist of basic respect. It is possible to perceive different endpoints to our logical conclusions and still behave well. It is even more critical in these instances to cultivate esteem for the other side, seeking an equilibrium by adding to situations instead of tearing them down.

Today, I will seek to be congenial when I have to put up firm boundaries.

Bridging the Family Divide

Often rooted in deeper divisions, our polarized society brings to the fore differences between us and our family members. We may not offer the level of understanding that we would to strangers, as our emotions are a tangled mess of preconceived notions and past hurts that strain to see logic at all. Our practice of unification must start with those who are closest to us. We must value them for what they are to us as opposed to what they say to us.

Today, I will be mindful not to sow deeper divisions between me and my family members based on differing opinions.

Are We Correct?

We are entitled to our individual beliefs, but they serve us best when verifiable facts support them. We must approach our rhetoric with a sincere mind which seeks to back up our opinions. The truth is the best salesperson possible. It won't need our help or embellishment.

Today, I will consider sources and verify the integrity of my statements to others.

Altruism

Our polarized society often deals in poison rhetoric that cuts to the bone. It refuses to compromise and works to tear down as opposed to building up. It is our responsibility to rise above the bombastic and recognize within other people opportunities for grace, mercy, and service. This works to find a place of maximum peace for everyone as we work for the well-being of others.

Today, I will move forward practicing benevolence.

Yes, I Do Care About Your Feelings

Today's divisive culture seems to work to display a cavalier and mean attitude toward the genuine sadness or misunderstanding others present. While we do not have to tear down reasonable boundaries and capitulate as a result of others' feelings, it is our responsibility not to needlessly compound situations with evil rhetoric. Empathy, when well placed, is memorable and powerful.

Today, I will work to build up others instead of tearing them down.

Can Middle Ground Exist?

By its nature, political polarization implies that there is no room to accommodate. We stand at our respective ends, retrenching our positions and discouraging those who would compromise. We vilify opposing experiences when, in reality, their total is just the sum of what has brought the other side to its conclusions. They may be sincerely and honestly held. An equally sincere and honest hand outstretched is essential for shared progress and is becoming more and more necessary for common survival.

Today, I will offer understanding and abandon mindless opposition.

Practice Compromise

Even when no overall consensus can be reached, the solution to problems can be found in the middle ground of compromise. This does not indicate capitulation but comes from the hard work of give-and-take and honest presentation of needs. It does not damage opposing viewpoints but instead finds a way forward. It is the antidote to a stalemate, and when done creatively, it can improve circumstances for both parties to a disagreement.

Today, I will commit to searching for a thread of mutual needs within conflict.

Do I Always Have to Have an Answer?

Polarization automatically counterpoints opinions expressed by others that we disagree with. We feel as though we must have answers ready whether or not they pass the test of logic. We behave most harmoniously when we admit that there is not an equal and opposing view where none exists. A non-reflexive intellect makes room for thoughtfulness and does not add to the cacophony. Accuracy is more important than a quick retort.

Today, I will remember that I do not have to demonize others when I am unable to explain my own views.

Is There Really Safety in Numbers?

Today's societal division seems to carve us into opposing mobs. It is easy to get caught up in the inertia of what everybody else is thinking and not consider things for ourselves. This can lead us to extreme viewpoints, which may ultimately marginalize us. Unity asks us to move in from the margins to form a grand consensus rather than creating discord.

Today, I will give issues careful thought for myself and not just mimic others.

Reach Across

Division forms a gap that widens over time. It is our responsibility to span this divide and extend a hand to the other side. This work must be done to preserve a society that has sustained us for decades. This doesn't happen automatically. We must show the ability to assimilate opposing viewpoints and make them welcome.

Today, I will extend myself to others to find commonality and reinforce common purpose.

Taking Empty Rhetoric at Face Value

Today's public discourse is driven by largely empty oratory designed to incite rather than inform. Feelings are not always indicative of truth, and a move toward unity requires us to understand one another's actual natures without static. The path to middle ground requires honesty and an ability to ignore chances to tear others down.

Today, I will strive to turn away from angry words that divide.

What Made Them So Different?

The chasm between us did not develop to these extremes quickly. The distance is the sum of neglect, misunderstanding, and lack of effort over time. It is the product of years of alienation. Hope is the integral force that can use communication to close the divide. It is the light that we can rely on to show a path to common ground.

Today, I will understand why those whose viewpoints oppose mine came to have them. I will work to be hopeful and move closer to unity.

When Our Leaders Do Not Listen

Effective leadership listens to all viewpoints and then moves forward. When our government is not responsive in this way, it is our responsibility to maintain a civil discourse that takes reason into account and refutes erroneous ideas. This can be done without rancor or drama and is simply an expression of our democracy.

Today, I will work to voice my opinions respectfully.

Eliminate the Barriers

We have picked sides and set up roadblocks. We have put too much distance between ourselves. It feels like a vast, forbidding river to cross. It feels like there is no guarantee. Even if we make the effort to cross it, there might not be a payoff. The distance pulls us away from one another with force. The way home is to shrink the divide. Everything that looks like a wall between us should be dismantled, even if it is just so we can see one another.

Today, I will try to remove gaps between me and my fellow humans.

The Part of Myself That No One Else Gets

We are all entitled to our innermost selves. At our core, we have a place around which we enforce boundaries and refuse to yield. Working toward harmony does not exclude our right to this. When we compromise, we are not capitulating. We are simply looking for solutions that work.

Today, I will honor myself while still seeking a workable middle ground.

Meet at the Simple Things

The search for the middle ground does not have to be a winding road. There are common feelings, common ties, and universal things that remind us that we are born of one spirit. Common ground exists in our love for children, the acknowledgment of others' achievements, and intuitive common courtesy. These are the basis for reinforcing our humanity. They are the solid ground on which we can build.

Today, I will look for the simple truth of others and affirm it.

Make Something Worthwhile

The move to the middle ground can result from attraction and not promotion. The power of solidarity can speak for itself in the form of practical solutions and improved outcomes. Each time we gain a new victory, the ground in the middle becomes more expansive as it is continually recognized as the place to be happy and whole.

Today, I will seek to play a role in building something that will be worthy of compromise.

Common Denominators

Whether we choose to admit it or not, there are common threads that run through our existence regardless of our allegiances. We all succeed, suffer, experience joy, cry, and feel from a common internal, eternal place. Nothing can truly defeat our sameness in these regards, and genuine unity is built upon them as a foundation.

Today, I will seek the common denominator in situations and look to preserve it and create from it.

Don't Insert Yourself

Beliefs are not universal. The energy spent proselytizing may be better spent pursuing our own path. Understanding, instead of correction, should be our goal. In this way, common ground can be an exchange of ideas as opposed to conflict. It can be the median that graciously allows a broader overall path.

Today, I will be mindful of respecting others' beliefs and willing to work with them rather than trying to change them.

A Loving Heart

Positive regard for others builds bonds and reaches across gaps in interpersonal understanding. While our logical minds dictate only the small degrees of compromise that we think we can tolerate, a default of caring with our emotional mind can infuse situations and move people back toward harmonious results. It embodies strength.

Today, I will be compassionate and promote love.

Contempt Before Investigation

Highly charged talk aimed at others fuels contempt as a knee-jerk, reflexive polar reaction. Division leaps to conclusions, while thoughtful examination of facts and mitigating circumstances supports unity. We make better points to others when we are deliberative.

Today, I will not automatically judge but will systematically seek to support my conclusions.

I Will Forge My Own Identity

Rancorous political discourse centers on strong personalities. Those who align with them seem to be signing off on both the good and the bad of their demagogue. Substance becomes secondary to identity. Unity dismisses this notion and replaces it with self-determination and an ability to respond to facts as individuals. It asks us not to just follow without thinking.

Today, I will be mindful not to follow the crowd to an illogical end based solely on a leader's persona.

The Culture War

Tribal influences pull us apart. We trade belonging for common sense and collectively turn a blind eye and a hard heart toward others. The move toward unity urges us to belong universally and not segregate. It is inclusive of all, not just our own group. It can give everyone the opportunity to be a kindred spirit, uplifting the whole.

Today, I will not exclude others and will be open to a universal bond.

Like Vermin

Division dehumanizes. Those who would seek to manipulate our differences push the poles ever further apart with old rhetoric that attempts to make us forget that we are all worthy. It aims to normalize cruelty and hatred. Unity insists that we understand them for the evil that they are.

Today, I will honor the dignity of others.

Issues Versus Emotions

Emotions lead us to catastrophize. It is easier to base a grievance on raw feelings than to think it through. Cooling down discourse can leave room for thoughtful explanation and facilitate solutions for underlying problems. In this way, we can become intelligent and effective.

Today, I will look beyond the visceral to identify problems and work toward resolution.

The Reality Check

Exploitation creates chaos that pulls us away from the truth. Lies seem real, and the outlandish narrative carries us away. We long for a singular story that explains everything simply, but it can be hard to find a narrative without embellishment or gaslighting. Harmonious truth lies in the recognition of facts and deliberative action in the face of complicated issues.

Today, I will turn away from simple but outlandish narratives.

Get the Poison Out

Our antagonistic lack of ability to work towards solutions leads us to sadness that eats away at our very core. We have to drain away the fuel of resentment. If we do not, it becomes a beast that grows arms and legs of its own and carries us away. Speaking our truth to others in a non-hostile way can remove indignation and allow us to heal.

Today, I will seek to remove sadness and diffuse sorrow.

No Violence!

Physical confrontation cannot be a part of a unified society. It is the wretched result of passion without love. It gains momentum, multiplies, and fuels anarchy. It does not offer solutions; instead, it sows chaos. A singular path to common truths is only available when we keep our hands and feet to ourselves!

Today, I will regard violence as the brutal end of hope.

Remain Hopeful

An earnest belief in unity is difficult to maintain. Events divide us irrationally and injure us, and it is easy to feel that there is no return. However, there is a way out of the woods. Hope lives in the outstretched hands of kindness and the unwavering search for love.

Today, I will steadfastly seek to enshrine hope within a loving heart.

Discomfort

The past is full of uncomfortable truths that demonstrate how we can disregard others to the extreme. These memories should not be forgotten. Teaching them is not indoctrination but a reminder of the wrongs of the past in the hope that they will not be repeated. Becoming better and eliminating wrongs does not disfavor any group but instead elevates us all.

Today, I will acknowledge history as fact and seek not to repeat evil deeds.

A Threat to Survival

While it may seem so, our secure place of relative peace and prosperity is not a guarantee. Division seeks to destroy us from within. A society founded on individual worth and choice cannot reserve these privileges for a chosen few without retaliation. Urgent action is needed to ensure that there is a place for all of us together in a working whole that remains intact.

Today, I will be aware of threats that might leave our society unable to cope, and I will be willing to work against them.

Backing the Blue

We are fortunate in our country to have police who protect us from harm and help us maintain order. This seems to have become a rallying point for those who would make too much of it. There are also rampant abuses and outright murders carried out behind the badge. While the police have necessary power, they are servants of the people and derive that power from all of them.

Today, I will understand the proper role of law enforcement.

Develop a Love Affair with the Facts

In a world where backing up "our truth" with facts is becoming increasingly difficult, it is our responsibility to seek them. They must be verifiable without reservation, immutable, and the result of our intuitions backed up with the work of a logical mind and a keen eye. Objective truth must be continuously sought. It is the antidote to chaos.

Today, I will seek facts as opposed to assumptions.

Offer Generational Love

Our society passes its character down through time. It is up to us to see that the content of this character promotes unity and strives to make the lives of those behind us better than our own. This result only takes consistent, simple acts that lead by example. It is this attention to the core of future generations that ensures our longevity and ability to move through any circumstance.

Today, I will do my best to teach love and thoughtfulness in a way that can be carried forward.

Take a Single Step

The fractures in our society can seem overwhelming. It is difficult to understand which direction to move with so many random "rabbit trails" available that seem to lead to nothing. The thought of them leads to overload and paralysis. Societal responsibility indicates to us that we should take a step toward problems anyway so that the solutions may reveal themselves. It is not necessary to understand the exact nature of this reciprocation; instead, we must know that it is available and move.

Today, I will internalize the need to make incremental progress that I can initiate.

Look Beneath the Voices

It seems today's fractured society has descended into a rancorous discourse that leaves no room for thought. Others are wrong simply because they do not belong to our group or share common circumstances with us. A society in need asks us, however, to look deeper and attempt to gain a better understanding which is not led by rhetoric. The move to a singularity of purpose calls upon us to have the presence of mind to ignore arguments designed only to fuel prejudice.

Today, I will make an effort not to judge by words alone.

I Need Your Opinion

Thoughtful solutions do not exist in a vacuum. We can build a better society with input from all sides. We do not have to agree completely. Instead, each new opinion offers additional fuel to stoke the fire of real and positive change. It can be the sum of our common experiences brought to bear to influence valuable, inclusive outcomes.

Today, I will seek to understand the minds of those around me and invite them to contribute to the common good.

Empty Air

Our automatic, instantaneous society demands continuous input to process. Our information sources hate "dead air." As a result, we have largely filled the vacuum with a stream of unverifiable facts and half-truths. We have lost the ability to enjoy the comfort of silence and its wisdom in making way for honest answers. Good ideas must have room to breathe.

Today, I will seek to internalize substance and ignore static.

The Perils of Service

Public service has become a minefield that few are motivated to traverse. The costs can feel too high to bear, as others who disagree can denigrate us to extremes that seem barely possible. This climate has to change. The path back to a unifying purpose must place ideas above personalities and integrity before expediency. This change in civil discourse can only be brought about through the sum of collective effort.

Today, I will be mindful of the humanity of those who serve us and work to show respect.

A New Narrative

Our divided society continues to write a narrative of chaos and uncertain direction. Our institutions seem dysfunctional, and at times, it appears that they are only advancing the story of what cannot be done. We must be the agents of change by speaking with our voices and our votes. It is up to us to be the seed from which a better narrative of cooperation and steps forward for the common good can grow. It is our individual responsibility to foster incremental change.

Today, I will contribute to a new story that is inclusive and effective.

Flexibility

Our current discord often clouds thoughtful and correct decision-making. Intransigent opinions stand in the way of moving the collective whole toward a better purpose. It is incumbent upon us to consider the views of others in the context of our own boundaries and absolutes and make concessions where necessary to find a way forward.

Today, I will be willing to listen to the reasoning of others and respond to it.

While We Are Not Looking

Extreme polarization is a stealthy force that seeks to destroy us. While we are busy slandering and smearing others, our institutions seem to be giving way to frustration and approaching anarchy at a rapid rate. The degree of tolerance for mistakes is becoming smaller. We must bring positive and inclusive change to bear. Failure to do so in the coming days will leave the realm of theory and bring us a stark reality.

Today, I will impress upon others the need for rapid positive action.

Redefine Character

Character is not defined by those who would dictate to us how to behave. It is also not another individual's capitulation to our opinion. Character is an individual, innate quality available to each of us based on our own experience and judgment. Its content is not universal, but its presence can be and is the raw material from which effective compromise is built. It does not exclude.

Today, I will work to separate character from dogma and seek not to criticize but rather to uplift others' beliefs.

Walk Away from a Bitter Heart

Intractability is the enemy of progress. Unfortunately, for many of us, life has left us with resentment that results in an inability to trust or compromise. The path to collective good requires these abilities. Those who show a repeated refusal to move toward them must, out of necessity, be marginalized. We must seek to love them from a distance.

Today, I will understand and be able to identify those who are unwilling to work toward unity.

Grace, Along with Victory

Too many avenues of our society espouse a "scorched earth" mentality. When one side wins, they continue to vilify the other side. They emphasize that victory is everything, not leaving the foundation for common ground for another day. Inclusive society insists that we leave a clear pathway toward reconciliation and a road wide enough to accommodate everyone within the new normal. This allows for peace with honor for the other side.

Today, I will be mindful of placing my victories in perspective.

I Can't Believe They Did That

Some actions of others leave us astounded. Whether they occupy an untenable position or simply lack regard, it is often hard to believe what comes out of people's mouths or accept their actions. Even though these things make it hard to be conciliatory, there is no chance for a unified society if we do not figure out how to understand fringe behavior, accept it for what it is, and move forward.

Today, I will work to suspend disbelief and move on from the unexpected or unexplainable.

Keep an Eye on the Prize

Our return to civility in society will take patience and endurance. Rather than getting caught up in the moment's potential losses, we must understand them as part of a big picture that overarches circumstances. They are temporal, and tomorrow is another day. Achieving the goal of a society that benefits all makes the strength that remains after defeats genuinely worth reviving.

Today, I will be mindful of the goal of unity and resolve not to give up.

From the General to the Specific

Those who would control seek to sow confusion. Generalities are the order of the day. They are designed to keep us from looking deeper and identifying individual elements of problems. They prevent solutions. One size does not fit all, and it is our responsibility to understand that there are specifics in every situation. They must be sought and addressed.

Today, I will ignore the smokescreen and develop my own informed opinions.

Don't Give Polarization Power

Extremism feeds on fear and a lack of understanding. The more we give in, the deeper its hold on us. We have a choice in this regard, however, as we can turn toward centrist thoughts that leave room for middle ground. We can foster positive choices and act to reconcile differences before their simple inertia pushes the poles further apart.

Today, I will be mindful not to fuel division but to understand the value of unity.

The Unseen Conspiracy

It is appalling how many different theories exist to explain grievances, real or imaginary. The standard for proof has become much lower than in the past. These theories are often nothing but conjecture, and they just serve as a device to exploit division and a lack of respect for the intellect of others. At their worst, they are a grave and deceitful danger.

Today, I will disregard the unproven and not allow my imagination to further divisiveness.

Shrink the Distance

The common ground lies somewhere between us on the political spectrum. When the gap is wide, finding the spot of peace and understanding seems foreign and daunting. If we do not feel we can get there in a given moment, at least communication and regard for others can make the division smaller. They are creative, binding forces over the long term.

Today, I will summon the courage to work toward common ground, even when others seem distant and unreachable.

Love Versus Judgment

The intrinsic value of love gets lost within polarization. Division accentuates differences, and we do not bother to reverse course and attempt to understand and offer regard for the thoughts and feelings of others. Even though we usually have incomplete information, we become judgmental and push others away, harming the cause of a collective society in the process.

Today, I will strive to take the time to be more understanding and to offer love.

Believe in a Functional World

Division leaves us feeling as though nothing works anymore. Our institutions are strained, and what we once considered orderly falls into chaos. The move to the middle ground requires faith and a willingness to apply patience as we work for change. These virtues can allow us to restore workable norms and confidence in them.

Today, I will continue to work within institutions to foster responsiveness.

Information Is Power

Accurate, timely information is still a necessary commodity. Our ability to move forward depends on the detail and veracity of the opinions we base our actions upon. Those of us seeking lasting unity must gather as much vetted information as possible before making decisions. Common ground requires a firm foundation. We must gather, fact-check, and then act accordingly.

Today, I will respect the power inherent in the truth.

My Values and Your Values

Our principles and ethics may not be universal. The content of our conscience is an individual thing. Your morality may not be the same as mine. Finding a way forward often requires understanding that others may have a different worldview. Unity insists that we incorporate these differences into spiritually viable solutions.

Today, I will seek flexible principles that maintain my boundaries but still allow progress.

I Still Have a Voice

Events move past us at a rapid pace. We feel less and less heard, and it is easy to develop a callous disregard for our ability to initiate change. If we express our truth, however, our voice can join a potential chorus that is big enough to move circumstances and inspire others. Shared truth is the very essence of unity.

Today, I will remember to speak up and embrace the chance that my voice will influence results.

Why Do You Say You Hate Me?

Sharp words and bad attitudes are sometimes part of the generalizations others make about us, our group, and our agendas. It feels like automatic dislike and contempt before we even have an opportunity to be seen as ourselves. The road to the middle asks us to understand this mechanism that divides us and to seek to work past it to dispel the erroneous impressions of others irrefutably.

Today, I will try to give others grace and accommodate their attitude until they reach acceptance of me.

Use the Power You Have

We can feel insignificant. We can feel devoid of strength, especially as compared to the forces we perceive arrayed against us. We must still, however, be willing to exert individual and incremental power to give the thought of common ground credibility and a substantial base. In this way, we find that we can move our part of the mountain.

Today, I will not discount my ability to exert influence as an individual.

Join Hands and Face Outward

The cause of unity asks us to meet in the middle with like-minded people and then offer a more substantial result to others. We can hold it up to the light, and it can provide a beacon for those still seeking a better path. While not proselytizing, this effort can potentially win others over to our collective point of view. It will allow us all to be closer to powerful agreement.

Today, I will be mindful work toward consensus and then spread its message outwardly.

Practicality

Our judgment as to what works and what doesn't work should be based on a realistic and unbiased view of our abilities. We cannot dismiss actions within the search for common ground as impractical just because they are hard. We must review our capacities and be willing to give of ourselves to gain ground. This remains of value even when we fall short of our goals.

Today, I will be sure that I am doing all that I can to further the cause of unity.

Can We Ever Get There?

The task of moving toward common ground seems daunting, and we wonder if we can even accomplish togetherness as a restored norm. Returning to it insists that we have faith that actions still bring about results. Nothing is impossible if we approach problems with an open heart and mind. The resulting love can be contagious.

Today, I will seek to fortify my belief in change.

Why Can't We Talk?

The lines of communication have been shut down by emotional, all-or-nothing thinking. Simple discourse feels like a lost art in the face of others who are unreceptive figures. The return to civility and a workable middle ground depends upon our ability to open dialogue. This is the fundamental first step forward.

Today, I will not deny my ability to talk about issues in a controlled way.

Be Where Your Hands and Feet Are

The work for change occurs in the here and now. It cannot be projected into a future that we cannot predict. It must be the product of an honest assessment of our position at this moment. Above all, we must be present. Developing the middle ground requires the actions of industrious hands and moving feet.

Today, I will be mindful of the immediate task of unity that lies in front of me.

Unity within Public Discourse

The common good can only arise in the absence of contempt between opposing sides. Even where there is sharp disagreement, it is still possible to be respectful of the opinions of others in an open forum. Treating others with emotional integrity allows us to "agree to disagree." This leaves communication open and harmony possible.

Today, I will strive to hold others in positive regard and control angry rhetoric.

The Shape of Change

We must be willing participants as we author new norms. Our world of change for the better must include a universal effort to develop something sustainable. We move forward, discover new contours, and form the foundation upon which good can evolve. This is fostered by a belief that unity and our best days lie ahead.

Today, I will understand that my everyday actions are shaping the possibility of a better world.

Listen, Then Speak

A new, respectful society is predicated upon our ability to listen first. Automatic responses shut everyone down, and we never hear solutions because they remain unspoken when people don't feel heard. The middle ground should be a thoughtful place of reconciliation and growth. It must be a space for considered expression that, by default, arrives at a listening ear.

Today, I will take full measure of the feelings and ideas of others before I speak.

We Have Done This Before

Today's situation is not the only time that our country has been divided. Over the course of years, we have regularly alienated others over views regarding class, race, and the use of military force. While resolutions have not been perfect, society has maintained itself through periods of near anarchy. While today's division presents unique challenges, our track record has been to persevere.

Today, I will seek to understand the adaptability and strength of our society.

Judgment Versus Discernment

We can differ in opinion without judging others as evil or deviant. Our ability to discern facts and likely outcomes does not have to be a pronouncement on the worthiness of others. Instead, it can be a guide for actions. We can be astute without being condescending.

Today, I will understand that I can determine good next actions without being self-righteous.

Turn from Hostility

Anger has become an unwelcome feature of our political discourse. Emotions take precedence over policy, and personalities become outsized and overtly defensive. A return to the middle ground requires us to turn down the temperature. We must acknowledge universal humanity and show others respect.

Today, I will maintain a calm demeanor even in disagreeable circumstances.

When Logic Must Prevail

Emotional minds paint situations with a broad brush. Misplaced sentiment can be a stream rushing forward, carrying us away from common sense and dignity. Polarized problems require the application of logical solutions that are grounded in fact and integrity. We cannot simply turn our backs on reason, regardless of the causes we espouse.

Today, I will seek to bring emotional problems closer to logical solutions.

Repair, Don't Demolish

Bad experiences seem to prompt some to tear down everything and start over. Many of us have given up and seek to destroy the status quo. This ignores the likelihood that something worse may be erected in its wake. While change is inevitable, it must be thoughtfully constructed and incorporate the best of our old society and hope for what it can become.

Today, I will not hasten change for its own sake.

Dissolving Stereotypes

Stereotypes are an inaccurate shorthand when we try to put others in perspective. Group members are not "always" a certain way. There is divergence and individuality within groups, and we must meet each person and situation in context and on its merit.

Today, I will not paint people or situations with a broad brush. I will seek to understand nuance.

They Are Not an Abomination

Our social discourse has moved to extremes. It seems we can't merely dislike anymore; we must hate. This hatred is based on allegiances and not on personal knowledge or any sort of interpersonal intuition. The move to the middle ground is predicated upon avoiding these extremes. Polar differences in opinion must not automatically vilify the other side. They must merely seek to add diversified ideas to a discussion.

Today, I will simply disagree with others when necessary.

Identity Politics

We have become a culture that places personalities ahead of true substance. Leadership seems to come to those who can make the biggest noise and not those who have the most astute things to say. This feeds on ignorance and a lack of motivation to gain a deeper understanding. We must value meaning and seek to embrace it.

Today, I will not simply give my allegiance to the loudest person.

Value the Act of Doing Your Best

Division is demoralizing. It feels as though the poles grow ever wider apart. It is easy to let go and give up, thinking that we will not affect the outcome regardless of the actions we take. The cause of unity requires us to continue to do our best even when we do not see incremental change.

Today, I will continue to contribute my best to society and allow it to find its value.

America Strong

We have seen evidence that it can take tragedy to bring our fractured society together for good. Duress leads us to examine the most basic commonalities of love, loyalty, and regard for one another. It pushes us together and can unify us. When we band together for a common ideal, we show the best of our innate strength. This power is available to us even without calamity.

Today, I will understand that we are at our best together in the face of adversity. This is proof of our inherent abilities.

Separate Science from Denial

We have become divided in the face of cold, unyielding facts regarding our environment. We are slowly making our planet uninhabitable, and this can be empirically proven. To come together, we must understand that this is not a hoax or a power play but a genuine emergency. While those who deny this should be respectfully heard, this denial must be refuted as we try to move together to meet existential threats.

Today, I will admit to the integrity of science even when it contradicts my lifestyle.

Revere Community

Our fractured society must begin to pitch a more expansive tent, open to all of our neighbors regardless of opinion. While we are bound to disagree, a new reverence for the act of coming together despite conflict must be valued as we attempt to move forward as a whole. Unity must become a default from which differences are settled.

Today, I will seek opportunities to strengthen my community and its diverse inhabitants.

What Would Love Do?

Doing the next right thing is a full-time job. This statement, however, lacks the moralism that gets overlaid on it. The "right" thing is subject to so much interpretation. It is infused with the color of "shoulds and oughts" that we assign to it. It becomes the product of the influences of too many others. Love in this context can guide us to mercy in its purest form, not subject to interpretation and merely useful in the moment.

Today, I will work to have love break all ties in my thought processes. I will rely on it for guidance.

Maximize Regard

Our regard for one another has never been absolute. Polarization emphasizes differences in society, but even in the most unified of times there have been different shades of love in the face of truth. As we return to the middle, we can rest assured there will still be uneven places. These can be mitigated as we find compromises and solutions.

Today, I will try to learn to love others to the degree that I am able as we approach unity.

Offer the Raw Material of Change

Division makes us weary and nonproductive. Emotional responses to this can slow us to a stop just when the need for fresh ideas and new leadership is greatest. Our collective power can bridge the widest gap and solve problems. Even in times of struggle, the sum of our creativity can make a difference.

Today, I will be mindful to put forth my best as I contribute to a successful society.

Hang Out with the Winners

Those who value rhetoric over getting things done plant and cultivate the seeds of division. Opinions without substance are everywhere, trying to drown out solidarity by their sheer volume. While unity asks us to consider the views of all, it is necessary to identify and turn away from bombastic attitudes that would drag us down. We must recognize the attitudes of others that we cannot change and move on to those that we can.

Today, I will try to base my interaction with society on logic and avoid those who hold consistently negative views.

The Foundation

While its extremes have recently taken us down a dark road, diversity of opinion and the individual's entitlement to it are the very basis of our free society. Even though division and acrimony seem to rule the day, our right to peacefully disagree and compromise to achieve solutions is a sacred trust.

Today, I will remember that respect for opinions is at the very root of our democracy.

Participate

We seem to live in the politics of hopelessness. It feels useless to try to move the needle through individual action. Our effect on outcomes seems small, and we are not sure our voices count or are even heard. An effective society insists that we maintain faith in our institutions and exercise our ability to contribute. Not doing so is to surrender to chaos. We must be willing to be collective instruments of thoughtful change.

__Today, I will make it a point to participate in our society by working to restore faith.__

Underlying Reasons

Current conflict is often the product of past bad experiences. We can honor justifications for what seem to be immovable opinions. When these precursors to behavior are attended to, others can feel heard and accepted and be willing to compromise.

Today, I will work to understand the past through the eyes of others.

Admit to Myths

Truth is the light by which we can be guided toward consensus. This light is extinguished by mythological problems invented in the self-interest of others. These problems are often designed so that the other side has to attempt to "prove a negative." Doing this is impossible, and asking for it is counterproductive. We must be willing to look for the truth and embrace it when we find it based on the best evidence available.

Today, I will be genuine and not perpetuate lies that harm the greater good.

Feelings and Compromise

The journey to a common good calls us to seek wisdom and logic. We should not allow our emotional minds to take control. We must strive to advocate fervently and emotionally rather than simply obstruct. Our losses can be learning experiences. This can only happen when we are open to possibility, removing contrary and reflexive reactions as a default.

Today, I will understand that my emotions may not align with a correct truth and that I must yield to accurate solutions.

Repairing Trust

Our divided society leaves in its wake hurt feelings and betrayal. The "other side" seems untrustworthy. Perhaps they have proven themselves as such through deceitful and even traitorous actions. A return to unity, however, calls upon us to allow others to make amends and regain our confidence. While this process can be halting at best, perseverance and a willing heart can prevail.

Today, I will not completely close my mind and heart to others regardless of their past deeds.

Acceptance

Our deteriorated discourse can leave us in disbelief. It results in a treacherous path of problems that seem unworldly and foreign to us when judged by previous norms. The road to common ground, however, directs us to accept facts and circumstances just as they are at this moment. Only then can we find a way forward.

Today, I will meet divisive challenges by embracing circumstance.

Don't Force Values

All of us have experienced different paths to the present. These have developed within us innate ideals of right and wrong and of acceptable thought and behavior. While this seldom leads to consensus, unification has more of a chance when we respect one another's beliefs and resist the urge to enforce our values upon others.

Today, I will maintain an open and understanding mind.

We Must All Win

In our fractured, competitive, and capitalist society, the "haves" and "have-nots" look at one another across a deep divide. Victory within these circumstances looks different to each of us. Our struggle for unanimity, while perhaps not reflected in comparative dollars and cents, must afford each of us the opportunity to thrive and survive in our own contexts.

Today, I will be mindful of others' situations and seek to enhance their triumphs.

Be a Place of Refuge

Automatic black-and-white opinions leave no gray area, no refuge. Views that would find common ground are sometimes not voiced as they seemingly have nowhere to take root and be nurtured. Open arms and an open heart can provide a glimmer of hope where it feels like none exists. They create dialogue.

Today, I will be outwardly welcoming and receptive.

Promote Reform

Our ability to make things right is at the center of our ability to unify. When the status quo does not serve both sides of an issue, it is incumbent upon us to point out inequity and work toward the common good. This is not troublemaking but rather an invitation to others to join us in sensible solutions.

Today, I will seek to move the common good forward and work to enhance it.

Possibilities

Our rhetoric can leave us buried in hopelessness and unable to see progress. The synergy of ideas and action, however, can lead us to strength. Even at the height of negative results due to our division, it is possible to combine strategies and work together to move forward and bring about positive change. This is only limited by our willingness.

Today, I will be eager to find the best possible solutions and zealously move toward the highest ground.

Civil War

Divisions in our society are so great that some people think a literal civil war is imminent. While there is significant dissent and disagreement, the term war implies irreparable damage that can only be solved by violence. This is the most extreme measure available. Unity asks us to turn from this sort of highly charged rhetoric to a path of reconciliation.

Today, I will promote peace even among those who disagree with me.

Value Understanding

Our segmented society does not seem to spend much time listening to others or processing what they say. We jump to conclusions and act accordingly. Conversely, deep listening and a true understanding of others' situations can help us reconcile actions and build a common bond.

Today, I will seek to understand the deeper context of conversations.

Don't Give Up on Them

We may feel hopelessly separated from those whose views diametrically oppose ours. We can tend to write off relationships and take the path of least resistance. While strength and resolution may come slowly, they are worth working toward and waiting for. These resolutions become an inclusive foundation for a future that adapts to circumstances and is not quick to judge.

Today, I will attempt to persevere and mend broken connections.

Be a Part of the Answer

Division and obstruction have become defaults in our ruptured communities. Inflaming differences has no value. It only makes our conflicts more chaotic, and nothing gets done. Solidarity can come from a sincere effort to be open-minded, to listen for common ground, and to act upon it.

Today, I will seek to provide value and not subtract from solutions.

Speak Up with Courage

Change and reconciliation only occur when we have the bravery to understand and point out systemic difficulties. If we do not do this, things that don't work will continue to move forward in error and send us deeper into division. A well-placed sentence or impassioned plea provides a spot from which problems recede and answers affirm.

Today, I will dare to speak of dysfunction so that it may be repaired.

Indignation

Indignation is the raw material of hatred. Instead of speaking of our grievances and diffusing ill will, animosity held inward causes us to deny compromise and push people further away. The thought of solidarity invites us to address the feelings and character of situations before we sort out the facts. The exercise of speaking the truth about our feelings without rancor provides fertile ground for new growth. It disarms division before it becomes a hateful extreme.

Today, I will remove the chip from my shoulder.

Be Inclusive with Intent

When we only offer our best to our own tribe, there is no room for civilization's diversity to provide answers from its collective mind. The ominous scope of our problems requires that we invite all solutions. We must stretch out our arms to encompass all who have something to offer. If we are intentional about this, it will soon become a default that promotes better and more rapid solutions.

Today, I will seek to add the presence of others to enrich situations.

Lean Into Resolutions

Our road to common ground cannot be followed to its end with empty professions of intent devoid of action. We must put the force of our perseverance and imagination behind them. We must not give up and work to solve difficulties with consistency and effectiveness. In this way, we gain respect and maintain focus.

***Today, I will be resolute in the pursuit of mutually beneficial actions that yield effective results.**

Ask Don't Tell

We can only discover a path to solidarity when we take the trouble to understand the content of others' minds. It is impossible to know this if we do not inquire. Contentious situations can be diffused if we seek clarity instead of making demands based on faulty knowledge. A listening and inquisitive ear convinces others rather than commanding results. This simple respect is vital to unity.

Today, I will actively ask questions to gain more complete knowledge of the nuance of circumstances.

Learn Where to Stop

Division loves to have the last word. Sorting out conflict generally involves uncomfortable truths that we must understand and swallow. Our desire for unity asks us to refrain from the spiteful retort and instead offer constructive action-based strategies. They are the path to harmony that is not destroyed by a combative attitude.

Today, I will hold my tongue when necessary to allow situations to end peacefully.

Greatness

Greatness is not something that we have won or lost. It is the concept of being American in its finest sense, combining differing viewpoints from diverse sources in order to synthesize a way forward. It exemplifies love, strength, and freedom. It is present within all of us. It is not something to exploit rhetorically.

Today, I will honor quiet victories. They are the American spirit.

Believe History

From the Civil War through the Vietnam era and beyond, our society has persevered and found solutions at what seemed to be its darkest and most divisive hours. We have gone to great depths but have always navigated rough waters to remain resolute in maintaining freedom. Our resilience has been tested in this way and always triumphs. This is the great lesson of our history.

Today, I will look to the past to draw strength for the present and future.

Solution Not Division

Problems demand resolution, not empty rhetoric. It can be easy to paint issues with a broad brush that does not analyze detail but rather moves along with the mob. It is our duty within society to turn to thoughtful reflection rather than insult and lead with a logical mind rather than emotion. Actions must be grounded in solutions.

Today, I will do my best to bring people to the middle ground of considered and effective results.

Move Past Bad Faith

Today, the trespasses and dirty dealing of the past leave us wary of others and their motives. We get so used to lies and half-truths that we believe they are an omnipresent default. Truthful unity asks us to overcome uncertainty and evaluate individual situations on their own merits. It asks us to take things at face value in each moment, giving the benefit of the doubt until proven wrong.

Today, I will do my best to keep an open mind, even with those who disagree with me.

Vulgarity

While defined differently from person to person, there is a common ground that recognizes the disgusting and shameful. Standards of love, empathy, and trust dictate a move away from words that further anger and divide us. Good ideas thoughtfully exchanged move us closer to solidarity and a better day.

Today, I will remove shocking and crude dialogue from my exchanges with others and seek to uplift instead.

Repairing the Smallest Systems

Our societal whole is the sum of its small parts. Even tiny actions carry inertia as they move either toward or away from common ground. Our ability to truly fix what is broken on a macro level lies in the micro details of one-on-one interactions. Overlooking nothing is the surest way to develop a firm foundation for a new normal.

Today, I will pay attention to detail and not take things for granted.

Keep the Good Ideas

Divided society and divided government seem to operate void of the ability to find inclusive consensus and a way forward. All-or-nothing instincts lead us further away from the value of give and take for the common good, even within victory. Truly valuable ideas get swept away in a winner-take-all culture where the losers are entirely ignored in the rush forward. Seeking accommodation, on the other hand, allows blended results that last and prove their efficacy.

Today, I will keep the best of the intellect of others.

Accusations

Vilifying the other side of an argument only serves to bring about bitterness and defensiveness. Nothing can grow in the middle. The peaceful comparison of ideas without recrimination leaves fertile ground for unity. Accusations push people further away from one another.

Today, I will not disparage others.

Human Issues

It is easy to objectify the other side. Sometimes, we lack commonality of experience. Other times, we simply cannot muster enough objectivity to put ourselves in their shoes and look beyond prejudice. It is easy to lose sight of the fact that even the most contentious disagreements involve human beings with thoughts, feelings, and needs. The journey to improvement begins with understanding them.

Today, I will strive to apply inclusive empathy to situations.

Spirituality in Sheep's Clothing

Our spiritual responsibility, while it includes others, is ultimately to power greater than ourselves. Extremes only serve to distance us from our desire to be unified with this gift. Some people would divide us to keep us from fully experiencing the harmony inherent in this search. This act is often only for temporal gain, as their version of "universal truth" usually leads us to a particular political party or candidate and away from an individual choice of spirit and conscience. Unity asks us to see through those who would proselytize us away from a common good based on love.

Today, I will resolve to move closer to my own true spiritual path and away from division.

Aren't We Still a Community?

We must live together. Despite all the semantics and disagreements, there are common needs for protection, sustenance, and mental well-being. These are universal, regardless of the moment's rancor. They are an essential bond, and they form the basis of unity that respects all.

Today, I will work to see beyond past disagreements, discover common necessities, and address their requirements.

Exploitation

Division leaves us feeling used. Opportunists see one pole or the other in our public psyche and work to exploit division for their own ends. When we are at our most vulnerable, their way often seems like the path of least resistance and a source of support. Practical harmony, however, results when we think for ourselves and look past those who would try to capitalize on circumstances.

Today, I will be mindful of those who would profit from discord and develop my own beliefs.

Step Away from the Fringes

Right and left can coexist. To do this requires the ability to compromise and to turn our back on extremism. A lack of reason often accompanies extremes. We must abandon the emotional and seek to find wise, logical solutions in the middle ground of common sense and fair-minded discourse.

Today, I will seek to walk inward toward others and away from the edges.

Allowing Emotion

The quest for a middle ground can feel like an either-or proposition. To allow our logical minds to saturate with the truth and knowledge needed to get there, we think that there is no room for pure emotion. We may believe that our feelings betray us. Instead, our emotions can be used for unity, letting others know the strength of our convictions and sincerity in finding common ground.

Today, I will strive to show others my authentic self as I work to move us all forward.

Can We Win Them Over?

Our division demands absolute agreement from others, with no room for dissent. We seem to have turned our backs on others, assuming that everything is set in stone. The middle ground demands that we give up on making others walk with us in lockstep. Alternate roads can lead us to common ends. Love and liberty are best served when we remain diverse. It's not about winning them over but about winning together.

Today, I will concentrate less on changing minds and more on making the sum of ideas greater.

Shine a Light

Charisma is often mistaken for substance, for possession of one clear truth. While charismatic messengers present as all-knowing, the best in our leadership shines a light that others simply follow. It does not claim all the answers, but it is a beacon powered by the resonance of clear thought as a way out of the darkness.

Today, I will allow myself to be shown a way out of disharmony and discord and will follow an illuminated path.

Allow for Transition

Polarization has come to us over a long time. At its most acute, we strive for instant answers that rectify wrongs immediately. While we may be tired of hearing about incremental change amid injustice, the move to the middle ground must be supported by a logical but rapid progression that is not disruptive in and of itself.

Today, I will strive for the patience to allow change to occur effectively.

Be Less Sanctimonious

An area of painful, concrete division in our society is the unquestioning belief that we alone have the path to the one true God. There is a frightening synergy afoot that claims that one cannot have a valid relationship with God if they are part of an opposing political party. This thought is short-sighted and is part of the cancer that spreads to push us apart to the extreme of no salvation for anyone. We cannot question the lives of others as spiritual beings and expect to live in harmony. Unity insists that tolerance is essential for our mutual survival.

Today, I will seek to validate the beliefs of others.

Invest Faith in a New Beginning

Our divisions leave us feeling hopeless. We scan for places to initiate common ground and become discouraged when they are not readily apparent. We must convince ourselves, however, that acts of reconciliation are still available and are not pointless. They are crucial to bridging gaps that allow the whole to survive and flourish.

Today, I will work to maintain a mindset of optimism that seeks solidarity.

Can This Be Real?

As the poles of our society push farther out, events become surreal. We ask ourselves how we got here and feel as though we are along for the ride in a fantasy land where anything evil can happen. While reality breaks new territory, those of us who desire unity must work to effectively and inclusively address the harm caused by outliers of behavior and deal with their aftermath.

Today, I will not allow the simple shock of events to place me at a standstill.

Don't Let Sadness Take Over

We get discouraged, and some give up trying. The effort toward common ground, however, implores us to continue to work toward moving forward. Even one thoughtful voice can move the needle, and the sum of many voices can move the mountain.

Today, I will remember to articulate my desire for good.

What Do I Hear?

Information we gather is run through the filter of our experiences and beliefs. Mixed messages abound. What passes through our ears tends to be a stream of chaos. It can be hard to hear the call to a clear path. The road back to unity, however, requires us to be discerning and seek the common truth that benefits all of us. We can persevere.

Today, I will do my best to be astute and seek a common thread amid the noise.

Necessary Compromise

The least effective means of conflict resolution involves holding out for everything we want. There are likely plausible justifications on the part of the opposing side for certain things. Wisdom may be contained in these. It is incumbent upon those of us who seek unity not to defend a hard line for its own sake. We must also send a message to those in power when they try to do so.

Today, I will honor compromise and hold those who reflexively refuse to do so accountable.

Teaching Government Its Role

There is serious and wide-reaching disagreement over the place our government should take in society. Its authority is derived from the people, but they are far from one voice. We must find and articulate common ground to ensure that extremists do not control the levers of power.

Today, I understand that the power of my government is not absolute and needs my direction.

When Love Doesn't Feel Like Enough

Family members find one another on opposite ends of the spectrum, and underlying love can be overshadowed by what feels like the only logical progression in our minds. Perpetuating love, however, insists that we continue to have faith in our abilities to include and compromise. We can return it to its place as the common denominator and strengthen ties.

Today, I will seek to understand the elements of non-contentious love.

Be Less Cunning

Being genuine takes effort. It is an effort well spent, as being less beguiling leaves more room for truth of spirit. It is difficult for slickness and sincerity to coexist. We should not seek to lure and trap others, but instead, we should enlighten and give them power to use for the common good.

Today, I will strive to be authentic and credible in a way that invites others to the middle ground.

Listen Actively

The road to the middle ground is contained within what other people say. Beneath the surface of rhetoric, there can be a core of genuine need and sincere desire to move forward. Even the words of those who would be adversarial often give clues to a subtext that is not as divisive. Getting together requires that we seek this underlying meaning.

Today, I will seek to listen first.

Respecting Work

Within our work ethic lies the sincerity of our convictions and our willingness to give our effort to them. If we respect this quality in others, our regard can translate into a synergistic effort that moves us away from pretense and toward unity. If our sweat and tears are directed toward the common good and away from division, this can become a ready and powerful force.

Today, I will be willing to acknowledge the abilities of others and seek to be inclusive of them.

Let Go of Desperation

People tend to make poor judgments in desperation. The drama of the moment seems enormous, to the point where the drama itself becomes bigger than what's at stake. The middle ground seeks to relieve anxiety and urgency. It moves forward thoughtfully.

Today, I will not let the dramatic character of situations get the best of me.

Passion

Modern discourse seeks to lead too much from a careless but impassioned mindset. It feels like nothing is deliberative, and the snap judgment or easy insult takes the place of a thoughtful position. Conversely, too much movement toward logic does not correctly take feelings into account. Commonality asks us to find the equilibrium between the two. It is the common ground that can elevate everyone.

Today, I will do my best to set an example that reflects both heart and intellect.

I See Myself Within You

At its most basic, common ground is made up of diverse people who love, think, work, and believe. While we maintain individuality, these activities form the basis of who we are. Individuals can become like-minded when we appreciate similarities in these deep forces and seek to operate from a unified consciousness.

Today, I will strive to recognize similarities between myself and others and use them to enhance common goals.

Discuss, Don't Divide

Communication can help dissolve divisiveness. We come to issues from different sides. That does not, however, mean that we cannot initiate practical discourse. Even disagreements can bear the fruit of a better way forward. The more we talk, the more we can develop the middle ground together.

Today, I will not be divisive by default but will seek to talk through problems to resolution.

Morality

We do not have an individual corner on righteousness. What is holy has many definitions. Regardless of the deep sincerity of our mores, unity asks us to temper our dogma and respect the behaviors and beliefs of others. Love can be the common denominator that embraces substance. In this way, we can arrive at a middle ground together.

Today, I will be mindful and inclusive regarding the beliefs of others.

Dysfunction

Our opposing views have left us debilitated and lacking functionality. It is hard to see the way forward, so we just stop. At every turn, we seem evenly divided with no tiebreaker. Unity, however, demands continued faith in compromise. We must believe that the adamant and obstinate can give way to a reconciliatory place of peace.

Today, I will not hold on to opposition for its own sake.

How Can They Really Know Me?

We have constructed walls around ourselves, fortified by the safety of numbers inherent in mob mentality. We are convinced that no one else can see the exact nature of our individual troubles. The move to a better society is built upon the sort of openness that can allow others past our defenses to foster genuine cooperation.

Today, I will strive to be vulnerable in a way that allows moving forward together.

Just Like Me

Some things are universal. As divided as we are, a thoughtful and gentle hand can erase gaps. Leading with love takes us by the hand and moves us to common ground. Seek to find the ability of others to stand with us in the common ground of a smile, a touch, a knowing glance. Turn toward those things and away from automatic thoughts that push us apart.

Today, I will seek to find the common ground of love.

Understanding the Hearts of Others

Everyone comes to this moment in time from a diverse path. We build upon our experiences and shape our abilities, and this becomes the core of our existence. Passionate disagreement stems from deeply held beliefs that we mostly come by honestly through the course of living. The combination that unlocks common purpose is the ability to understand why people feel the way they do and what can be done to work within their needs.

Today, I will work to include deep empathy in my actions to honor others and move forward.

Give of Your Best

Compromise is often obtained begrudgingly. The temptation is not to give our most conscientious effort when the results have not reflected our heart's desires. The unified path forward works best, however, when we are aware of this and intentionally offer our strongest intellect and hard work. This builds good faith.

Today, I will intentionally put special interests aside.

Legacy and the New Normal

We seek to leave an example for those behind us. As opposed to a fractured view, the singleness of common purpose leads us to construct shared new norms. These norms can become the solid ground from which the future grows. They foster the generational hope that there will be less division, less hatred, and more reliance upon love and unity.

Today, I will seek to leave hope of mutual benefit in my wake.

Removing Half Truth

We tend to reflexively cling to "our side of the story," which often deviates from what actually happened from an objective view. Our temptation is to present only the parts that support our polarized thoughts. The journey to common ground demands that we face the truth squarely and allow its facts to shape mutually beneficial outcomes.

Today, I will be forthright in my analysis of facts. This understanding will guide me as I look forward.

Actively Abandon Division

Too often, we reflexively discount the experiences and thoughts of others and give way to lazy demonizing of what we don't understand. Polarity does not happen accidentally and is the sum of thousands of little pushes away. It takes being mindful to counteract this automatic response and willfully select another.

Today, I will be mindful to turn away from divisiveness.

Justice

In an effective society, no one can be above the law. While extremism may dictate an unbalanced approach, the scales of justice must remain even for all of us. This is the bedrock standard that must be observed. Unity dictates that we honor this core value without giving in to undue pressures or influence. Justice is not a weapon. It is an equalizer.

Today, I will work toward supporting legal order as an absolute.

Common Goals

Prosperity, health, and happiness are universal desires of the heart. While there may be disagreement as to how to obtain these, this commonality of purpose helps us find a middle ground on which everyone can be uplifted. Joining hands, instead of picking sides, is the most efficient way to well-being.

Today, I will seek to collaborate with others.

Accept Your Role

Moving our society back toward common goals requires that we each shoulder responsibility. The act of building a consensus requires willing participants who can face difficult choices and compromise. It will take all of us to move our culture toward undivided norms. We must take our place as agents of change.

Today, I will be willing to do my part to normalize cooperation.

Value Your Neighbor

Common ground becomes possible when we treat our neighbors with respect. A deep community is a fertile place from which consensus grows. Harmony informs decisions that benefit the whole and identifies actions that make us all stronger. It is the support for progress.

Today, I will appreciate my neighbors and enhance their ability to join me in forming a better society.

I'll Meet You in the Middle Ground

The wise middle ground can seem distant. We can feel as though we take steps toward it, but those aren't reciprocated, and we wind up short of the ideal. This leaves us frustrated, blaming, and too tired to keep up the walk. We take for granted that the gap will be there forever. We can defeat this by constantly inviting others to meet us there. We can show our willingness to embrace a universal good and our desire to share it.

Today, I will ask others to join me in a common purpose.

Making Room

Polar viewpoints, by their nature, leave a lot of middle ground uncovered. The more we consider giving others a seat at the table, the more likely this vacuum will be filled by hope and an opportunity for a better way forward together. This begins with the simple act of inclusiveness.

Today, I will seek to incorporate the thoughts and hearts of others as the raw material from which to build a middle ground.

Take a Step Toward Change

There is an adage that says, "If we take a step toward a problem, the solution will take a step back toward us." We must begin the journey of unification. Taking the first action may be the impetus required to overcome problems and prompt others to offer solutions. It removes barriers, shows good faith, and reaches across divides.

Today, I resolve to take an initial step directly toward common ground.

That Was Yesterday

Today's challenges must make us face forward in united, helpful thought. Past wrongs and injustices are undeniable but must fade in the light of new togetherness and fresh solutions. They should not be forgotten; to do so would risk repeating them. Our memories should, however, be tempered with peace, integrity, and solidarity as we seek the best present we can create.

Today, I will work toward leaving old wounds behind.

Promote Peaceful Change

Changes do not always need to be brought about by force or rancor. They can be the product of sincere collaboration, of the spirit of cooperation that recognizes the sum of parts as being greater than the whole. This new paradigm can become the norm, building a conduit for orderly progress. It moves toward solutions and walks away from conflict and division.

Today, I will be mindful that thoughtful change can bring about tranquility.

Rising Above a Melancholy Past

The past has left us with sad chapters, failings, and a blind spot for the possibilities of healing. Past wrongs may even bring us to tears as we recall the direct involvement of those close to us and their losses. Our personal icons are revered in the warm cloth of the righteous and exalted for their parts in what may have objectively been "the good fight" of the past. It is our responsibility in the present to acknowledge that we can rise above even a beautiful struggle. We can create something better.

Today, I will honor the past and look forward to a more inclusive future.

Learning to Disagree

Disagreement does not mean that the other party to the dispute has no value. It is not a license to vilify them or impugn their character. Doing this roils the water as we approach future conflict, as it then becomes more about personalities than logic. The need for consensus implores us to disagree well so that we may talk again another day.

Today, I will not burn bridges.

False Narratives of the Past

It is easy to take a nostalgic look back through rose-colored glasses. The "good old days" were seldom perfect. Their memory can take on a distaste for change that tries to drive the current narrative. Most progress is predicated upon change. We must seek to debunk myths and recognize the maladaptive parts of the past.

Today, I will stay in the present, where solutions are found.

Walk with an Open Heart

We tend to push away what we do not understand. It is easier to categorize than to think. If we take time to reflect, we can see that others are not adversaries but teachers. Taking the middle ground can save us from expending the unseen energy it takes us to hate and create the conscious power of love.

Today, I will seek to look beyond the surface and understand.

Peace as a Default

Peace is the atmosphere of the common good. It permeates effective decisions and guides direction toward future solutions. It is also a learned state of being. When it replaces conflict as a default, progress occurs.

Today, I will seek to lead with serenity.

Stop Keeping Score

Wins and losses are not the only measure of success or failure. The path to consensus in society is a balancing act of both, tilted toward mutual good and away from divisive failure. Results are more important than victories. Unity insists that this remains the focus.

Today, I will evenly evaluate outcomes.

Can We Still Be Reasonable?

Our rhetoric has been so divisive for so long that it is easy to lose sight of reasonable common truth. It tends to blur in the onslaught of strong opinions and personalities. Things have become so polarized that it does not seem that a middle ground can even exist. We must defeat this fallacy. At the heart of the desire to meet in the middle must be the internal assurance that reason can be regained once there. We must understand that logical thought and intellect are still present and can defeat demagoguery in its arena.

Today, I will assert that everyone has the capacity to be reasonable if they attempt to do so with intent.

Persevere

Our current division is the sum of many slippages, disregard for others, and adversarial thoughts and actions. When we begin the journey back to the middle, it may not feel reciprocated or well received. Despite this, we must finish the work. The middle ground is worth our patience and effort.

Today, I will work to remain on the task of reaching out to others.

About the Author

The path to service took a lot of turns for author John L. Walker, causing him to bring a unique experiential perspective to his writing as well as his practice of psychology. He graduated from North Texas State University in 1983 with honors with a BBA in Banking and Finance and then became a bank vice president at the tender age of twenty-five.

He left corporate life, however, and entered the music business, becoming a nationally touring singer/songwriter at thirty-two. His first wife died from substance abuse the year he turned thirty-seven. This formative experience was the catalyst for his departure from "the road."

This then led to the establishment of MacHenry's, an acclaimed entertainment venue for both touring and local music acts that Walker founded in his hometown of Fort Worth. It became a beloved hub for musicians, in large measure, due to Walker's ability to bring people together for a common purpose.

After MacHenry's closed, John realized that service to others would be a lifetime pursuit. As a result, he returned to school at fifty-two and obtained a master's degree in counseling from Tarleton State University. This made possible the establishment of Empathy Source Counseling in 2017, his private practice in suburban Fort Worth.

John has developed a track record of helping others through life experience and loss, concentrating on the treatment of grief and substance abuse. This work has led him to believe that true, lasting change begins with each individual. His cognitive behavioral approach has been incredibly effective, helping others apply considered thought and positive action to their difficulties.

His book *Breaking Common Ground* further embodies this approach, as it presents others with a personal means to overcome the hopeless societal division many of us feel. It is a basic, action-oriented approach to unity. It leverages proven strategies and is offered as an extension of a giving heart, a desire to be of service, and evidence of a loving, insightful perspective.

John now lives west of Fort Worth in Mineral Wells, Texas with his wife Glenda and their bossy cat, Emma.

www.ingramcontent.com/pod-product-compliance
Lightning Source LLC
Chambersburg PA
CBHW062147080426
42734CB00010B/1592